Jolliffe

E. McCullough.

1982

47

6c Da £3-49

PIERRE CABANNE: Jean-Louis Barrault as Hamlet

JEAN-LOUIS
BARRAULT

Reflections
on the
Theatre

WITH ILLUSTRATIONS
BY

Christian Bérard, Balthus, Maurice Brianchon, Pierre Cabanne
Lucien Coutaud, Jean Hugo, Félix Labisse, Jean Denis Malclès
André Masson, Mayo, Étienne Bertrand Weill

THEATRE BOOK CLUB
48 OLD BAILEY · LONDON

Translated by
BARBARA WALL
from the French Edition
first published by
JACQUES VAUTRAIN
Paris, 1949

THIS EDITION

First published for the THEATRE BOOK CLUB in
1952 (by arrangement with Rockliff Publishing
Corporation Ltd.) as one of the outstanding books
of the theatre selected for their members to whom
it is issued exclusively at a privilege price.
Particulars of membership can be obtained from
the offices of THEATRE BOOK CLUB, 48 Old Bailey,
London, E.C. 4

MADE AND PRINTED IN GREAT BRITAIN BY
SPOTTISWOODE BALLANTYNE AND COMPANY LIMITED
LONDON AND COLCHESTER

Foreword

ONE day in the winter of last year Jacques Vautrain came and gave me a commission. It was, he said, to set down on paper some of my reflections about the Theatre. As he wanted these to be handed in at the end of May, and as we were then in January, I promised to obey—given such a distant date-line.

But I was not in fact able to get down to Vautrain's project until June.

Then some months elapsed between the handing in of the manuscript and the arrival of the proofs, and already I had changed my mind about several things and altered various passages. More time elapsed between my sending back the proofs and receiving the printed book.

By then I had changed again . . . but this time it was too late. "I could not spend all my time tinkering with the text."

Where the theatre is concerned, then, time matters. The theatre is the art of the ephemeral, it is in continual flux: indeed the theatre is the symbol of all those successive deaths that we strew day after day by the wayside.

What we are and what we think to-day differs from what we were and what we thought yesterday while giving no inkling of what we shall be and shall think to-morrow.

If there is a place where we "never bathe twice in the same water" (as Heraclitus said) it is certainly in the theatre.

Change is our function, which is why we cannot be blamed for sometimes thinking differently from our elders, and it is also why we shouldn't be distressed if our juniors already think differently from ourselves.

With the theatre it is always "forward march".

PARIS, *September*, 1949.

v

Contents

CONTENTS

Part III. 1946–1949

viii

List of Illustrations

ix

LIST OF ILLUSTRATIONS

To follow one's inclination . . .
so long as it rises.
ANDRÉ GIDE

Dabbling in what one doesn't know,
with the help of what one does, is divine!
PAUL VALÉRY

The man who has a strong arm
and who breathes deeply of God's air,
there is no risk of his sinking.
PAUL CLAUDEL

1

The Young Player

ALL my life I shall remember that winter's day in 1931. That Moment, that very second—the march of the whole universe seemed to have come to an abrupt standstill—when I walked out of the Collège Chaptal and followed the Boulevard des Batignolles, when I crossed the *places* Clichy, Blanche and Pigalle and passed in front of the Médrano with its whiff of horses, when I panted a little climbing the narrow Rue Dancourt and when my heart suddenly decided to stick in my throat as I stood in front of the Atelier, and when, finally, the Atelier concierge, Madame Verny, who was so kind to me later, led me to Charles Dullin's dressing-room.

Was it really me or was it someone else? Oh, it was me all right; indeed it is me, for by the recurring quickening of my senses I know that it could still be me.

I wish we could keep a permanent hold on those waves of feeling that engulf us, those virgin emotions that make us almost want to faint.

To preserve, to cherish, as if it were the most precious thing, a *permanent virginity*. That is my first reflection.

My task here is not to write my memoirs, which would be premature, so much as to extract from a rapid recapitulation of the years some moral stock that will enable me to set out afresh on the right foot and armed with a new spirit.

I have adopted the chronological method for this book because it seemed to me the simplest, clearest and least 'artistic'. I don't want to make a literary work; I want to make my point.

What more reasonable than for a sailor to say to himself: "I left that place on such and such a day, landed there on another, there on another, and to-day I have arrived here. So let's make an inventory of our remaining provisions and set our course in that direction."

The purpose here is not to talk about oneself, but simply to recollect oneself so as not to be lost.

The memory of yesterday exists only so as to serve to-morrow.

Action is at its strongest when it is spontaneous; but spontaneity is fertile and fruitful only when based on well-digested experience. Hence I ponder my past experience so that my will to action shall be free from the 'reaching after reason' that has such a weakening effect on it.

That young man of twenty, striding along the boulevard an hour before the time of his appointment, yet hurrying for fear of being late; wearing a soft hat not his own, a suit that has been given him, a tailored top coat also a gift, and holding gloves too narrow to put on in his hand; with emptiness behind him and the thick mists of the future in front of him that his straining eyes are seeking to pierce; that young man . . .

Well, the memory of that young man is of use to me to-day in that he reminds me of what an audition is. Yes, he helps me to receive all those other young men who now come to me seeking an audition.

On that day everything to do with me was both clumsy and touching. Since then I have come to see that typical young men always are both clumsy and touching. And if a young man comes into our presence to-day with a conquering air and offhand manner that sometimes irritates our forty years, and if his gaucherie tempts us to react like an old man by way of protest, then we must remember that beneath that awkward air and off-hand manner everything is as tender as tender meat, as brittle as an egg-shell. Our forty years will have learnt nothing if they fail to realise that they must act with the greatest care—I do not say indulgence, but care. The care of the watchmaker who loves his watches. Youth has rights. But its zestful impetuosity is in conflict with young experience. It is for us to take the first step, for us to have trust. "Young men are young", as Molière said.

But first I had written Charles Dullin a letter, the rough copy of which by chance I kept. I must say it is pretty silly.

Sir,

I am a student aged twenty, a pupil at the École du Louvre, and so as to be able to paint I am an assistant at the Collège Chaptal where I received my secondary education.

But on the repeated advice of my friends and following my own innermost desires which for some time now I have known to be for the theatre (or the cinema), I would be happy to have the opinion, if possible, of some eminently competent person. . . .

To this end, may I ask you to grant me a brief interview?

Very much hoping for a favourable reply—if I am not putting you to too much trouble—I trust you will accept, Sir, the expression of my deep and respectful admiration.

Then, some days later, an answer came, not from Charles Dullin himself but from his private secretary, M. Priel. To the trite, uncouth letter from a penniless young assistant of Chaptal, of whom Charles Dullin had obviously never heard, Dullin, after some days, replied! That is why I feel such an infinite gratitude towards Charles Dullin. Who knows whether I would have persisted? At that time I was wavering between acting and painting. But all my painting aspirations had been foiled, whereas I make one overture to the stage—my letter—and I am literally sucked in as if my fate were awaiting me at the corner of the road, and this fate was nothing other than Charles Dullin's reply.

My whole life opened out as a result of this little summons, and to-day I genuinely believe that while I was pacing along the boulevard I recognised how portentous the situation was. In front of me was a black pit, but every object looming up beside me seemed to have a peculiar clarity as it does at night, while behind me, with every step I took, a fresh chasm was forming.

Dullin, then, had replied to my first raw letter. And he had done rightly. I entered his presence in a state of the most touching ignorance, and I think he was taken with my ignorance more than with my qualities.

I had prepared two scenes—one from *Les Femmes Savantes* and the other from *Britannicus*. And since I knew nothing whatever about auditions and about having to take someone to give the cues, I had learnt all the parts myself—that of Chrysale and all the *femmes savantes*, of Narcissus and Nero.

In his dressing-room Dullin was buried in a small armchair near the window yet not visible from the road, and his eyes were shrewd and amused. The lamp had been lit, for the day was drawing in. My gloves were still in my hand; I was far too nervous to put them down. I couldn't keep still for an instant but lurched to right and left like a great lout when I said: "*Et hors un gros Plutarque à mettre mes rabats*," and drew myself up stiffly like a shrew at: "*Le corps avec l'esprit fait figure mon frère*," etc.

Then I cast long black looks into space where my unknown partner should have been; long and charged with meaning:

"*Narcisse, c'est assez; je reconnais ce soin,*
Et ne souhaite pas que vous alliez plus loin."

A half turn, a glance shot at a lower level (for Nero should rightly be seated), a look of hypocritical surprise:

"*Quoi? pour Britannicus votre haine affaiblie*," etc.

I abandoned myself, naked, to all the changes of voice and attitude. While from the house opposite, which appeared to be a hotel of passage, a couple with nothing on was eyeing me, making harmless fun. . . .

At the end of this 'number' Dullin, perhaps moved by so much candour, paid me a few compliments in his teeth, and I understood that I might try to be an actor. He asked:

"Have you quite made up your mind to be an actor?"

"Yes, sir."

"You know that it's a very grave decision to make and that you will run the risk of starving to death?"

"Yes."

"Are you prepared to starve to death?"

"Yes, sir."

"And at the moment what do you live on?—for I'm sorry to have to tell you that one has to pay at the Atelier."

"I have no money at all, sir. I am an assistant at Chaptal *au pair*. I get my board and keep but nothing else."

"Then I will let you come to the school free. But don't tell anyone . . . if you do . . . well . . ."

And then I saw for the first time the Dullin that I was to imitate so often later, with the eyes of a martyr, the pout of a sulky child, rocking to and fro and selecting his small whining voice, the voice that always tried to sound so utterly pathetic. My theatre life was starting.

That was February, 1931. Eagerly I followed the courses at the school. Chaptal kicked me out in July. In September Dullin renewed his solemn questionings concerning my vocation for the theatre, and I answered more and more categorically.

"Very well then, that's agreed. You are now part of the company. You will get 15 francs a day and as a start you will learn the part of Volpone's servant. I shan't make any contract with you; we don't do that here. That sort of thing is all very well for business men, but with us our word is enough." And in fact I never signed a contract with Charles Dullin.

And so it was that my dreams were realised, guided by some fairy.

I made my début on the stage of the Atelier, in the part of one of Volpone's servants, on 8 September, 1931, my twenty-first birthday.

What reflections can I draw from this memory?

Reflections about the conditions of young actors nowadays.

What lesson can I learn?

B

The way in which I ought to behave with them.

I in my turn have often received letters from young men wanting to consecrate their lives to the theatre. Some of which were distinctly less awkward than my own. I have not always answered them, and hence I have not followed the example of my master. But I notice that I answer more and more often. I have learnt to answer and hence conclude that: answering is a thing to be learnt. The art of finding one's way among one's fellow creatures is slowly come by. If one is perceptive, one feels a second instinct, an acquired instinct forming within one: a sense that develops by slow degrees.

How to answer our fellow creatures without becoming submerged by them. . . . Our answer should be dictated by Reason. The heart is soft and too ready to overflow and thus causes a defensive reaction to set in whereby even if we want to answer we don't let ourselves. Only Reason can remain mistress of such a delicate situation. To answer without becoming submerged . . . and our fellows are voracious.

Answering the appeals that arrive! A quality slowly acquired. It is a science, like learning the science of loving.

There is another science one acquires slowly—that of loving one's art.

And that brings me to another thing I want to speak about: the young actor's love of the theatre.

When I discuss this with a veteran actor or producer I am very struck by the kind of bitterness—deriving, I dare say, from genuine disillusionment—with which the actor or producer makes his points.

"The young of to-day are devoid of passion. They think they love the theatre, but it is only so as to become known. They think only of the cinema. They are incapable of giving their work freely, for their art's sake. They have lost the faith. They giggle on the stage, arrive late for rehearsals and think they are too good for their parts. They never work at a small part. They want to have

PIERRE CABANNE: André Brunot in *Amphitryon*

7

the big parts at once. Their heads are turned by the lightning, abnormal and demoralising successes of certain young people put over as the 'discovery of the year' by the film industry. Where is the professional conscience of our young?" etc., etc.

To all these bitter remarks I invariably answer that the professional conscience is a science one acquires slowly.

The young people who embrace the life of the theatre to-day love their art fully as much as we loved it. Their passion is the same as ours was. They are fired with their art as much as we were. But, like us, they will take twenty years to know how to love it as we do now, and, like us, at the end of twenty years they will still have far to go to learn to love it more and more.

If a young actor has a giggling fit on the stage it is not a sign of indifference; it is a sign of unawareness, it is precisely a sign of youth.

When those two young girls of the Conservatoire, Marie Bell and Madeleine Renaud, were seized with uncontrollable giggles on the stage because Maître Silvain had his tunic caught between his buttocks, and when this nervous laughter had gone on for so long that they had to leave the stage—and that at the Théâtre Français—it did not mean that Marie Bell and Madeleine Renaud did not love their art; it quite simply meant that those two girls were like two puppies who upset their dish with their clumsy paws.

Why expect a young man to know how to behave? Not to know how to love does not mean that one does not love!

If it is true that the young actor of to-day has more cares, more worries, and is therefore more on the make than we were at twenty, the fact is easily explained. His life is more difficult than ours was; he has been deprived of *care-freeness*.

It is also easy to explain why many young actors of to-day are more materially exigent than we were. The uses to which some cinema magnates put the cinema falsifies the true art of the cinema.

Yet there is no denying that every actor should have some screen experience. It is perfectly normal that a young actor should be obsessed with the desire to pass in front of the camera.

As I see it there exists only one artistic profession for the actor: it is DRAMATIC ART.

But dramatic art to-day has several branches, whereas until the beginning of the twentieth century it had only one. To-day dramatic art includes:

The Theatre
The Cinema
The Wireless

and to-morrow:

Television.

A desire to make films does not imply a lack of professional conscience. He lacks professional conscience who wants to make films so as to be recognised in the street. But this sin against the professional conscience is usually committed by the young player who will gradually develop a taste for true cinema and as time goes by will recognise the futility of his first desire.

With the exception of some outstanding people who learn how to love very early, it is natural for a young actor to get to love his art slowly. The fact that it takes time does not diminish his power of love.

Hence the veteran actor and producer should not lament. Young people are just as keen as they were when they themselves were young. It is for those who have already acquired the art of love to lead the others and to initiate them by loving them.

If I were to make a brief diagnosis of the modern young actor this is roughly what I should say:

1. A certain drying-up of passion caused by the withdrawal from him, by the age in which we live, of the faculty of care-freeness. Our epoch has deprived him of the faintest possibility of living in a state of freedom from care.

2. At all times and always people tend to fall in with the superficial side of life, to jump to conclusions while avoiding causes. The drying-up referred to above brings out this tendency.

3. It must not be forgotten that the modern young are for the most part the children of 'failures'. The example of what their

parents have made of life is hardly likely to put them on the road towards wisdom, truth and virtue. Hence most of the time they have to fall back on their own intellectual intuition. Is it surprising if some of them take advantage of this?

4. Apart from the consequences that follow the withdrawal of care-freeness and the (excusable) mentality that comes from being the children of failures, the young seem to me very much the same as what they always have been.

Nevertheless I will here add a few words about a sentiment very dear to me, namely LOVE FOR THE OBJECT . . . for the object itself.

It seems to happen that we like the object that we make less and less for its own sake. We attach greater importance to the return we shall get from it than to its success on its own account; let us say, its disinterested success.

Often an actor answers a remark made him with: "But it won't be noticed." What does it matter if it is noticed or not? What matters is whether it has been done well or not!

This reproach does not apply to young actors only but to all ages.

When I was producing François Mauriac's *Mal Aimés* at the Théâtre Français it happened that in a certain scene the décor did not give the desired effect. There were only a few days before the dress rehearsal and so a quick solution had to be found. I decided to put the set on the slant. Like that it looked better and saved the situation. Now the stage, in the Français, itself slopes a little. The décor, tilted, leaned forward a little but from the audience that could not be seen. "It didn't show." Nevertheless, M. Jallerat, chief mechanic at the Français, was cast into deep gloom at the mere idea of doing a shoddy piece of work. "Enough to make one quit the trade," he said, almost in tears.

I fully understood his dismay. So I got his team together and took full responsibility for the arrangement, stressing the austere period we were going through (it was in the middle of the Occupation) and the impossibility of getting hold of canvas and wood to remake the décor from scratch. I did not want the chief mechanic to lose prestige in front of his team and I assured him of the exceptional nature of the heresy we were committing.

That day M. Jallerat gave a fine example of love of his craft.

Love of the object . . . for itself. Disinterested love of the material success of the object. A well-made object. For its own sake.

2

Volpone's Bed

There he lay in bed, his mind full of plans
HOMER

AND so it was agreed that I would get 15 francs a day,
450 francs a month. It was the 1931–1932 season. But the
material difficulties were such that we did not always get
our pay; sometimes we got only 50 francs a week. In fact, that
was a heroic epoch!

It was quite impossible for me to rent a room in town; indeed
I had to resign myself to having no lodging at all. A resignation
made all the easier in that it gave me a better excuse—heroic-
romantic—for sleeping in the Atelier with the consent of my
beloved anarchist master.

I want to say this, whether you will laugh at me or not: from
1931 until 1935, for four whole years, I never met Dullin's eye
without trembling with awe and the desire to be worthy of him.
From 1931 to 1933 I was his constant butt, as if he were sub-
mitting the boiler of a steam engine to all the explosion tests.
I endured his injustices to the limit—his loving injustices.

But one fine day, when he had gone to have his snack at the
Bon Bock in the Rue Dancourt with the half bottle of Bordeaux
that seemed to me a symbol of the Director's magnificence, and
I had worked out my menu so as not to exceed 9 francs, we fell
in with each other returning to the theatre. There were only about
a hundred yards to go. I didn't dare accost him but walked
respectfully on the kerb beside the gutter, he on the pavement,
stooping a little, his small peasant's eyes fixed on the horizon, his
slack legs . . . Then he said something to me, I stammered a

vague reply, and suddenly I poured everything out and told him my despair at pleasing him so little. He said:

"You want to do too well. That's why you do badly."

And from that moment he no longer treated me as his butt but as his young accomplice.

A master is a good master only in so far as the pupil lets him be a good master. The nourishment he brings you depends on the nourishment you let him bring.

It is the pupil who brings out the richness of the master.

I had brought all my love to bear on Dullin. And by this one stroke he grafted me utterly on to him. Dullin was a true patron in himself, but only on condition that his subject surrendered himself entirely. There is no master in the world who can improve another, unless that other has already given himself to him entirely. It is the disciple's trust that makes a man a master. It is the disciple's faith that makes the head of a company into a midwife.

Dullin's genius lay in the fact that he remained essentially and constantly an authentic human being, and that he could create around him an atmosphere of apostleship and of absolute artistic purity and integrity.

His life was not governed by specified or calculated rules of how to behave—in one way with his pupils, in another with actors of his own generation, in another with authors, and differently again with heaven knows who else. No! He was always himself, always integrated with regard to himself, weak and heroic, unjust and yet generous, a rake and a bohemian, cruel yet a friend, simple yet an old fox. His long past made him cunning as a serpent; yet, confronted with the future, he was like a child. An old campaigner ever new. . . .

So I left my little room in town and camped at the Atelier.

One evening, after the performance of *Volpone* (the bed of the Fifth Act remaining on the stage), I conceived the idea of sleeping in Volpone's bed. . . .

Everyone had gone off for the night and the concierge had shut the doors. I was alone in the building. I crept, an intruder, on to

Pierre Cabanne. Jean-Louis Barrault in *The Trial*

14

the stage, found a stump of candle belonging to the manager, lit it, drew back the curtains of the bed which, for the sake of his precious perspective, Barsacq, at that time a young décor-designer, had made about 5 feet long.

I lay down.

The stage was there in the Silence. The arches were muffled with curtains. Bits of the décor cast ghostly shadows. The idea entered my head to pull back the great curtains. I wanted to feel the Presence of the auditorium. The auditorium peopled with seats and a whole potential public.

I pulled back the curtains as if I were taking a pleasure by theft. I took a step or two on the stage, the stage where I had been so frightened a short time ago. . . .

To think that in the Fourth Act, the tribunal Act, I was playing an officer and was barely capable of staying face to face with the audience lest I should faint with fear and my heart should break—what a fool to have such stage fright! I lingered a moment, motionless, on the proscenium. The Silence of the whole theatre possessed me. Layers of ice were upon me; everything froze around me; and soon I was submerged in Silence.

I was very near to being afraid and I went and cowered in bed . . . Volpone's bed. . . . There I dreamed and remembered.

My first impulse towards the life of the theatre goes back, perhaps, to my sixth year. I spent my whole childhood living imaginary stories and endowing all things with a human soul.

Even at that moment every seat in the stalls could have had its own personality for me; as it happened some were creaking (like me, they were dreaming). What a lot of things those seats have seen! The other day while knocking in one of the stage boxes to make another entrance, a love-letter was found between the boards and the wall, dating from 1840.

An old theatre of the outskirts of Paris . . . the life of all those actors and wandering players that Dullin had known. . . . It was in this theatre that my childhood dream was being realised. I was living the life of the Theatre. At that moment I was celebrating my marriage with the Theatre; and I perceived during that night of initiation that the whole art of the Theatre is to make that *Silence* vibrate. To unfreeze that Silence. To go against the current. When a river flows into the sea it dies; it flows right away into the communion of saints; its estuary is its sickness . . . so it is important to go against the current so as to get to the source, the birth, the essence. Art . . . the challenge to death. . . .

This *Silence*, studded with creakings in the magic enclosure, when only the inner sounds of my 'luminous' body, as Pythagoras put it, were audible to me, should never have left me; and I shall always have a picture of myself, crouching in Volpone's bed, passing my first deep night of love at the very fountain-head of my art.

Since then I have been in constant quest of that Silence, and from time to time I have happened on it—but perhaps in the middle of some scene flashing with projectors, in a white-hot dramatic situation, and in front of—or rather, among—thousands of people, a thousand listening human hearts, open, 'sharing', sharing the *present moment* with me.

So far, I have most often felt that marvellous sensation in Hamlet's great soliloquy, "To be or not to be."

When a thousand hearts beat in time with mine, and mine beats in time with theirs; when my heart's rhythm has set and will maintain the rhythm of all those other hearts; when we make ourselves ONE, then I can say that I know human love, I know love for a group of human beings, love between human beings. And, as at certain heights of love we may delay the moment of piercing wonder, so sometimes I delay the Moment. I remain quiet. I don't breathe; none of us breathes; we vibrate in immobility; and we discover that unique *Silence* which alone can give us the physical sensation of the *Present*.

The physical sensation of the *Present* filled with a progression of silence was to make its mark on me for ever.

That night was my first communion as an artist.

3

Elementary Education

To business that we love we rise betime
And go to't with delight.
ANTONY AND CLEOPATRA

AT the Atelier I learnt first and foremost to love the Theatre. We had before our eyes one of the greatest and sincerest lovers of the theatre you could meet with. The most instructive thing for us was simply to watch Charles Dullin at work.

As for acting parts, we didn't; I mean important parts. Small parts, yes; walking-on parts, utility parts. Often we played four or five of them in an evening.

Take *Richard III*. I remember I 'did', as they say, first a citizen, then Lord Grey, then the sheriff, then the second murderer, then the ghost of Lord Grey and finally a soldier. But with Dullin's example before us I can promise you that we explored the smallest, sketchiest part down to its most secret stronghold, its psychological depths.

He trained us to see the complexity of the smallest part. I swear that I have worked at the sheriff in *Richard III* as solemnly as if I were doing the part of Richard himself.

Every person who makes an entry on to the stage makes it in a particular *situation*.

What are his circumstances?

Where has he come from?

Where is he going?

What has he come to do?

What *object* can be found to *place* him from the first moment both for the public and for himself?

17

What is his shape, his outline, his cut? Has he a moustache, a beard, and if so how are they trimmed? Could he be married? What are his eating habits? What are his fads and fancies, etc.?

The sheriff became a problem comparable to King Lear. I took him so seriously that I made a mess of him from my first entrance; I fluffed my words and, nearly dying of fright, failed everywhere.

Dullin's teaching was based on the essential importance of *living a situation sincerely*. The exercises he taught us were practically always *exercises in sincerity*. We did not, perhaps, acquire a great technique but we certainly learnt to live the situation. If our words sometimes had a false ring, at least the sense of the true was within us.

My succession of small parts taught me, among other things, the art of make-up.

In Pirandello's *The Pleasure of Honesty*, in which Dullin was magnificent, I crossed the stage in the First Act as a nurse, clasping a bundle, for a baby, in my arms. Every evening I made myself up differently for this part. I designed my disguises myself and varied them. All of which enthralled me.

This brief entry over, I just had time to run up to the pupils' dressing-room, remove my make-up, and set to work on a new one, for at the end of the Second Act, indeed just as the curtain was falling, I was the third I don't remember what (a notary, I think), and for that part too I varied my make-up every night. On that particular make-up my fancy could roam to its heart's content for I knew that no one would see me. This is what happened:

One of the principals said:

"Let those men come in," and the servant opened the rear door. The first man came in: "Good morning, sirs." The second man followed, then the third—who was myself; but the first man's answer was the last remark of the Act and the cue for the lowering of the curtain.

Never once did I arrive on the scene in time to see even a corner of the auditorium. Always, when I arrived, the curtain had fallen.

I don't think another such restrained part exists in all the theatre's repertoire.

That did not prevent me from keeping my make-up on during the interval so that my friends could admire it—and Dullin, who was greatly amused.

I have said that the first thing we learnt was to live a situation sincerely. Next we learnt from what angle and in what spirit the theatre should be loved. We came to grips with the theatre through *purity*.

And if at the end of it all we couldn't do very much, at least we had learned what ought to be done in order to do well some day. We *learned*, rather than applied, a *method*.

Dullin's teaching drew attention to the body and its expression, to the religious meaning of the masque. Convention was irrevocably cast out, even if there was nothing to replace it. Which was what happened when the conventional, well-worn tones of tragedy, hollow and outmoded, were discarded with horror only to be replaced with nothing.

What choice is there between a bombastic actor who bellows the tragedy in an insensitive despair-making way, and the actor who seeks the true note of tragedy with the utmost sincerity but in vain?

All that can be said is that the first one's case is hopeless whereas the second perhaps has a slight chance.

The purity with which we were encouraged to approach the theatre was based on the far-away school of Stanislawski, on the nearer school of J. Copeau's Vieux Colombier, and on the fascinating theories of Gordon Craig.

To Stanislawski goes the honour of drawing our attention to the *faculty of concentration*, the *development of observation*, *self-control* and *decontraction*.

How on edge one becomes trying to decontract! It's quite maddening. And yet I believe in decontraction exercises. I shall give my method presently. I must say that for a creature so little gifted as myself in decontraction, I have attained a fairly high ability in it by now, though there is still so far to go!

I think the ability to decontract, if it does not come naturally, is one of the most painful stiles to cross in the life of the theatre. Mastering one's nerves: my God!

To Copeau goes the honour of raising the theatre to the level of the other arts; of restoring to our profession a certain greatness that hitherto had been the monopoly of the Théâtre Français.

To Gordon Craig belongs the honour of bringing home to us that our profession is a great craft, a collective craft. To share in the work of the stage-carpenter and the electrician, to help with the décor, the costume designs, to make up one's own face, learn a little if possible about the music, etc., etc. . . . to see the theatre as a Whole and not just a place for personal exhibitionism.

We didn't apply all these excellent maxims, but our minds were fed on them.

And yet it seems to me that we were taught a *method* rather than a *craft*.

Stanislawski's ideas came to us through his writings, *Ma Vie dans l'Art*, and so did Gordon Craig's. Copeau's influence came to us chiefly through stories about him.

How François Vibert set me dreaming once by his stories of the Vieux Colombier! But we got it, too, through the Compagnie des Quinze, whose director was Saint-Denis, Copeau's nephew, and which was the only professional tangible result of a school of theatre. It is the only case that I have really known.

I owe one of my keenest joys of the theatre to the Compagnie des Quinze and André Obey: I mean the *Viol de Lucrèce*. When I saw the *Viol de Lucrèce*, I felt that I was seeing the solution of the problem for the first time.

The two narrators, Suzanne Bing and Bovério, seemed to me to give an example of true diction. The problem of the word seemed to me to have been tackled by them and by the author with the greatest candour and seemed to me to give the very best results.

The plastic problem seemed to me resolved by M.-H. Dasté, so beautiful as Lucrèce, and Maistre, a perfect Tarquin. The setting

seemed to me true, exact. The work struck me as nobly balanced·
It was vigorous and musical.

That Copeau should have had the audacity to go to Pernand
with his 'copiaux', his school, and that this school should have been
capable of producing a company like the Compagnie des Quinze
seemed to me a supremely encouraging example.

So the Atelier gave me the purest *method* for my work, and the
sincerest. Moreover, both with Dullin and in our relations with
the Quinze players whom we frequently saw, I was bathed in
professional honesty.

Technically we had few opportunities for making rapid progress, but morally what was grafted on to us was of the highest
quality. And that contribution I still hold to-day as inestimable.

It is comparable with the education received by a child during
the first ten years of his life.

The Atelier . . . a Religion.

It was through the study of the Body that I was to approach the
technique of the actor.

Étienne Decroux was one of the Atelier company and had
come from the Vieux Colombier. His friends were very fond of
him but always talked of him with a little sidelong smile. They
looked on him as an eccentric. And indeed he baffled me quite a
bit, too.

The first time he deigned to speak to me he wounded me to the
quick. I have forgotten his exact words but I know they were
highly unpleasant, if not cruel.

Some days later he asked me, in a discouraged and not-daring-
to-hope tone of voice, if by any chance 'bodily expression'
interested me. I suppose he expected me to shy off, like the others.
He had already caused many to flee! I answered that it did interest
me.

The following day Decroux gave me my first lesson in mime.

Decroux had picked up his first notions about miming from
the Vieux Colombier and especially from the excellent and

c

disinterested efforts of a woman to whom we owe much:
Suzanne Bing.

With Suzanne Bing, Decroux had especially studied masque
playing and he spoke of her with constant admiration and respect.

Miming enthralled me from the first moment, and I was the
more passionately interested in it as for the first time I began to
see what it meant to have a *gift*.

A virtue, exterior to yourself, that has been given you.

We feel a sort of irresponsibility when faced with this gift.
Usually there is a gap between what we think we bring and what
we actually put across; but when we have the grace of the gift, if
we bring 100 we put across 120! Yes, it is a grace that has been
given us.

It was undeniable that I was gifted in bodily expression. And
I say it so easily because I sincerely believe that we are in no way
responsible for the gift.

Decroux quickly passed on to me what he already knew; he
gave me the benefit of the work he had already mastered, and we
soon set to work together.

For nearly two years we shared an almost communal life.
Nudist and vegetarian. What fun it was and what laughs we had!

We calculated our meals in terms of vitamins . . . and money.
To get the necessary number of vitamins we managed, in 1933, to
eat for 4 francs 40.

1 kippered herring	. . .	0.95
125 grams of raisins	. . .	1.75
1 lettuce with lemon juice and fruit		1.30
1 coffee (at the Café de la Poste)	.	0.40
		4.40

I don't know what that would represent to-day; but anyway
our hunger was satisfied.

Sometimes we alternated salad and lemon juice with boiled
semolina.

Decroux had not smoked for two years. He was a puritan revolutionary. He cultivated the more-than-perfect.

Until that time Decroux had stood alone against those who laughed at him; then, for nearly two years, there were the two of us; and of those who laughed, and us, it was we who became the stronger.

We were unable to go on working together. Which of us was to blame? Perhaps neither.

We were wild and at large. Our incessant leaps dangerously shook the theatre boards. It took us three weeks to perfect the step called the '*sur place*', a step we have done so often since. Each performed in turn in front of the other, who criticised. We were complementary to each other. Decroux, with his sure analytical sense and exceptional creative intelligence, could pin down the improvised variations that I executed more spontaneously.

The problem of walking, just walking, engrossed us.

Nothing is more difficult than walking, and a man may be betrayed by his walk.

Our advanced studies in walking put me so off my stride that it took me a good ten years to walk normally again (and even now I sometimes . . .!)

One of the greatest cooks in France once confided to me that, of all dishes, the most tricky to do well was and would remain: the fried egg. The difficulty being to do the yolk in the same time that it takes to do the white. This can be achieved only on a flame as pointed as a candle's.

In fact it is the simplest things that are the most tricky to do well.

To read, for example. To be able to read exactly what is written without omitting anything that is written and at the same time without adding anything of one's own. To be able to capture the exact content of the words one is reading. To be able to read! To be able to write! To know how to commit to paper one's exact thought with the aid of words that falsify nothing and at the same time make the right *ring*, the same ring that resounds simultaneously in one's head. To be able to write!

To walk!

One man walks as though he were waiting for his feet to change their position. He stands erect, waiting. Then his feet, blindly, one after the other, lift themselves and land on their heels. And it is only when the man feels assured that his heel is firm that he ventures to take the step. This man does not walk; he lets his feet move him.

Another man's feet squint, that is to say they turn in. Another has spiral legs—a dancer for example. Dancer's legs seem to savour such intense joy in changing their position that they give the impression of being transported into the air. The man, above, follows them.

But the man who walks is a moving WHOLE. Walking is centred neither in the toe nor in the heel. It is centred at the level of the chest.

It is the chest, carried on the supple spinal column, that should express a will to motion. And beneath this will to motion the legs coast along.

It is remarkable that whatever point of the body one is concentrating on (so long as one concentrates on it enough) that point attracts the attention of the watcher. As if it were luminous.

The man who walks should not attract attention to his feet, nor to his knees, but to the front of his chest. It is, if I can so put it, the chest that takes the first step. The man who walks has made a decision to change his place, and the first thing to move should be the centre of himself: that hollow magical box thanks to which he breathes and which is upheld, like an emblem of life, by the supplest stalk in the world—his spinal column.

To begin with the man has pledged himself; he has faith in himself; he carries himself forward confident in the reflex of his legs. And his legs follow him, serve him; they billow beneath him. He is a man moving, not a man following his feet. The most forward part of his chest should never be outstripped by the tip of his foremost foot.

That, at least, is walking in its pure state.

PIERRE CABANNE: sketch for *Les Fourberies de Scapin*

25

Once that is mastered, all walks are permitted. Every man has his own walk, a walk that gives him away in spite of himself. The actor must work on the walk of his character. But the pure act of walking, like that of reading, writing and frying eggs, is the most difficult thing in the world to achieve.

If I had been asked at that time what my opinion was of the art of Mime, I think this is what I should have said:

Mime is the art of SILENCE. It is one of the two extreme points of pure theatre; the other extreme point being pure diction.

It should be executed naked and if possible with the face hidden by an impersonal mask. It should be accompanied by no sound, no noise whatever, its element being *Silence* and its music essentially visual. Hence any musical accompaniment to a mime is sacrilege.

The trunks indispensable to the naked body should leave the particularly expressive abdominal muscles exposed; and the side of the leg should be free to above the thigh.

The glance is directed from the neck. It is the bust that is the source of expression. A mimer has two points of vision—the eyes and the tips of the breasts, and a continual interplay of harmony and contradiction exists between these two pairs of eyes. Every gesture originates in the spinal column. Hence the mimer's first duty is to become aware of his spinal column, vertebra by vertebra. The movement of the limbs, the arms and legs, springs from the manner of their attachment to these vertebrae. It is this continual awareness of their place of origin that gives the mimer's gestures their style, their dimension.

Every gesture derives from two essential movements:

Pulling

Pushing

The focal point lying at the centre of the stomach, the navel. The whole of life consists in either pulling towards oneself, or else pushing away from oneself, and Oneself is the navel.

And if we set aside the two arms and the two legs, the bust loses nothing of its expressiveness.

For the limbs are the indicatives of the action.

I, the *subject*, is the flag composed of the spinal column and the respiratory box. It is the bust. It is the Self, the outline, the *attitude*.

The *verb* is the *movement* of the creature. It is the very action of the bust.

The *complement* is indicated by the limbs (arms or legs). They *indicate*.

Thus my body writes a silent sentence in space. Subject or attitude; verb or movement properly so called; complement or indication.

And if anything is superadded to this expression of the body it will only detract from the purity of an art that is essentially poetic and valid in itself.

Permanent Training of the Mimer

1. Exercise for total *decontraction*, equivalent to a purge.
2. Awareness of *isolated muscles*. Learning particularly how to contract a given muscle while leaving the others relaxed.
3. Awareness of certain *groups of muscles*.
4. Acquisition of a *muscular tone*—neither contraction nor relaxation.
5. Development of the *abdominal muscles*.
6. The notes around the *spinal column*.
7. Study of the *whip* represented by the spinal column.
8. *Sincerity* of *feeling*.
9. Development of *concentration*. Analytical concentration, respiratory concentration. Shifting points of concentration. Those luminous points, of which we spoke above, that draw the attention.

Objective Mime

In the art of the mime all objects are imaginary. The imagined existence of an object will become real only when the muscular disturbance imposed by this object is suitably conveyed by the body of the mimer. Study of 'counterpoise'.

Example: I carry a pail of water at arm's length. This pail of water will exist at arm's length only if my body mimes the counterpoise of this pail, that is to say if my body mimes the displacement in the opposite direction that I would normally make in order to keep my balance in spite of the pail at arm's length. Since the objects are imaginary the study of counterpoise will put the mimer into a position of disequilibrium: hence the inexpressive parts of the mimer's body must make the necessary modifications for concealing this apparent disequilibrium.

The study of counterpoise is passionately interesting and is the key to the so-called objective mime.

Subjective Mime

Or, the study of the states of the soul translated into bodily expression. The metaphysical attitude of man in space.

An intoxicating study which lifts you up to the level of religious art. When we were pursuing our researches into subjective mime we felt we were drawing near to Oriental actors; we felt that we were discovering all over again the plastic art of Greek tragedy.

A typical theme for subjective mime is the study of the theme of death. To begin with the material struggle of the body grappling with sickness, then a moment of suspension, followed by the long, slow journey towards the abstract; suddenly overtaken by the final stroke bringing with it a transfiguration in the inmost being and in the body, in which the problem of death resolves itself by a solemn gesture, symbolic and unique in itself, detached from everything, independent like a line of pure poetry —a pure lyrical gesture.

The mime comprises two kinds of plastic material: on the one hand the gesture which simply serves the action, and, on the other hand and comparable with the narrative parts of tragedy, the gesture which is a Whole in itself. The gesture which is in itself a poem. The gesture makes poetry.

The transition from one kind to the other being comparable to the transition from prose to the alexandrine.

The more we delved into the mime the more resources it seemed to have.

What treasures we unearthed! Mime rapidly became one of my passions. It will always be one of my passions. Alas that there were so few people who really understood it. Hardly anyone appreciated it then. The rehabilitation of the art of mime will take a long, long time, several generations, but . . . "the beauty is not hoping for a thing; it is knowing that one has got it for ever", as Prouhèze says in *Le Soulier de Satin*.

Those were my first steps in the art of mime.

That was my elementary education.

4

As I Lay Dying

This fever called Living.
E. A. POE

SINCE entering the Atelier school I had had no other concern but rehearsals, Charles Dullin's example, the problems
posed by my studies, and my researches with Decroux.

I had been given a method for work, I had espoused a Spirit,
I had approached the technique of the actor through bodily
plastics.

The inside workings of the Theatre enthralled me. I can truly
say that my only joy at the evening performance was when the
fall of the curtain really proved to me that I had embraced the
career of the theatre.

Because at first I knew none of the joy I subsequently knew in
acting to and with the audience: I was much too frightened. For
a long time every performance was a ghastly ordeal.

At the beginning of the '34 to '35 season Tania Balachova lent
me a book by an American writer that had just been published.
This book was to engross me throughout the whole year. It was
As I Lay Dying, by William Faulkner.

That was a real 'encounter', and I am quite sure that it was the
only book I read that year.

The theme was admirable and through it I could express my
own opinions of that time. I don't think I saw things quite in this
light then, and if now I see *As I Lay Dying* as a sort of manifesto,
I certainly didn't think of it like that at the time.

The book absorbed me, and in my turn I put all my energies
into absorbing it.

In *As I Lay Dying* a certain wild young man tames a horse
wilder even than himself. Now this horse appealed to me from

30

the miming point of view. So it was from the point of view of the horse that I worked at *As I Lay Dying*.

But the whole atmosphere of the book was utterly seductive to me. The action took place in silence. There was no dialogue. The peasants didn't talk to each other. They operated in silence. They spoke only when alone. And the monologue seemed to me essentially dramatic. To talk to oneself is an emotive action, and quite necessary. Perhaps talking to someone else is too, but only "on condition that it is not used as a subterfuge to explain a situation to the public that the actors are incapable of conveying by their action". That was my opinion at that time.

In any case, with Faulkner's peasants there was no danger of their putting themselves out to explain the motives for their conduct to their contemporaries. Their climate was always that famous *silence*, the silence of Volpone's bed.

From this work which lasted six months there emerged a mime play which lasted nearly two hours.

We were just about to finish the '34 to '35 season. I had inherited 10,000 francs from my father's estate, and with this I decided to hire the Atelier from Dullin for six days at the end of the season, and I set about to find sympathetic colleagues. The play—excuse me, the spectacle—required fourteen or sixteen players, and the cast was made up solely of the faithful.

My thanks to all those comrades who put their trust in me, for it was needed!

Felix Labisse, whom I had not known long, did the décor and the costumes, bowing to all my exacting demands.

Tata Nacho, the Mexican composer, whom I had met through Desnos and who was particularly versed in Mexican and Mississippi folklore, wrote the music for us. . . . Just voices with no other accompaniment than a tambourine used by the actors on the stage itself and within the action.

I worked morning and night.[1] In the morning on the

[1] It was at this time that Pomiès, dear Pomiès who was to die so young, was working at his dancing in the basement of the Atelier.

proscenium in front of the curtain I availed myself of the light required by the charwomen who always cleaned out the theatre at that time.

I was much too far gone in enthusiasm to be put off by their presence and I worked at my horse in the briefest of trunks. And it was because of this that I received, from one of them, one of the most encouraging compliments of my life.

I was naked, having only my trunks for covering. Naturally no accessory could possibly indicate the presence of the imaginary horse that I was trying with all my might to tame.

In my passionate earnestness I quickly forgot the good women who were stacking up in baskets the rubbish left by the audience of the night before. The muffled noise of their brooms didn't worry me at all. One day, however, my attention was arrested by something. I stopped and saw that one of them had planted herself in front of me, leaning on her broom-handle. I realised at once that she must have been gazing at me for some minutes. I looked at her a little embarrassed, as if somehow at fault. She didn't budge but went on staring as if wanting to think her thought out.

We both felt rather idiotic.

Then I smiled, and she said; "I've been trying to figure out what you've been up to all these days on that horse of yours. . . ."

What a victory! What joy! What encouragement! What a spectator that woman was! What a reward!

The day of the dress rehearsal drew near. A young journalist, André Frank, had already become deeply interested in the thing. André Derain, on the other hand, who had recently done my portrait and to whom I had mimed the whole play and who had seemed interested, after coming to one rehearsal never put in an appearance again. . . . And his support could have been of considerable moral value, for his judgment had great influence with me and I admired him deeply.

Some of my colleagues lost heart and had to be replaced. The work had to start over again. Others stayed on but with waning enthusiasm: the departure of their friends demoralised them.

At the Deux Magots they were already beginning to joke about it all. The rumour went around that we were all stark naked. And indeed it was true. Those with the mentality of Rimbaud's 'Sitters' who are usually those with the most 'wit' easily found the appropriate words to belittle our efforts and make us look silly.

I had failed to get permission from the Authors' Society to use the real title of the book. As most of the action consisted in burying the corpse of a mother, I had named the piece *Autour d'une Mère* which the little pals of the Deux Magots quickly christened *Autour d'une m. . . .*

In short, apart from the sincere confidence of the young journalist André Frank and the unshakable faith of my two or three trusty friends such as Desnos and Labisse, and what remained of the cast, the pre-first-night publicity was pretty laughable.

One afternoon when we were rehearsing we heard some unaccustomed creakings from the circle and we suddenly realised that Charles Dullin was having a quiet peep at us. Was he for us or against us?

My great strength lay in the fact that it had to be done. The whole earth could fall to bits in a formidable final cosmic quake, but I firmly believe that I would still, in space, be rehearsing the taming of my horse.

The day of the dress rehearsal arrived . . . lamentable . . . general and complete discouragement. Charles Dullin, tenderly, had been present and when the rehearsal was over his discomfited look told us everything. The cast, dispirited, faded away and I remained with him alone.

He asked me if the following day we meant to do the play to the Press. I said yes. He said: "You'll forgive me if I don't come; it would be too painful."

I was at my wits' end; I was cruel, even insolent. I would have killed father and mother if necessary with a madman's calm. A state of mind I have always miraculously recaptured at every important first night, and even at every important moment. The salutary drug of frantic work.

The result no longer mattered to me. By and large I believed in the work I had done. I obeyed a sort of fatality.

When one has gone beyond the limits of fatigue one sleeps well. First thing in the morning the concierge woke me up with a telegram: the girl who had the principal part of the mother had suddenly fallen ill (?) and would not be able to play that night. I did not try to find out the cause of her illness. I thought only of the performance in the evening: the performance before the Press and the 'little Paris' vanguard led by the Deux Magots.

No! Not even that! Really I saw nothing but my own need to go through with it; in front of the Devil or the Pope, but go through with it.

I got up with "the formidable calm of reserves that are about to come into play" (as Saint-Exupéry has put it), and I went to wake up Labisse. I told him what had happened. For a minute his face implied that everything was finished!

"What do you mean to do?"

"I shall do it even if I have to act it all myself."

After a minute I repeated that I would do the whole thing alone if no one else wanted to go through with it.

"At that rate," he said, "why don't you act the mother?"

"The mother, as well as the son? But they have scenes together."

"That's true," said Labisse.

"What time is it? Ten. Then I've time to re-write some of the scenes."

"And this is how you'll dress," went on Labisse. "Naked to the waist, mask with a great black mane of hair on top, and we'll simply cut the mother's dress to make it into a wide skirt. . . ."

We separated. I sent everyone a telegram and went to re-write the scenes. I was not at the end of my strength. In the afternoon my comrades were thoroughly depressed and treated me as if I was mad. I insisted, and in order to convince them had to treat them to a thorough-going audition and give them the whole play in its new form.

Happily—and this is the moral of the story and my only excuse for committing it all to paper—necessity made us discover the true character of the mother.

The mother up till then had been just like all the other characters, just as human, no more human; but by the addition of the mask and this rig-out—naked male torso over a wide skirt, black mane of hair like those shrunken Mexican heads stuffed with sand —the character of the mother became a kind of idol like a totem, and raised the theme of the drama up to the level of tragedy.

The mother was about the only person who spoke, and she spoke only after her death.

While alive the human beings operated according to their individual passions and in silence. Once death had been crossed the word became possible, and this strange character moved about among human beings with a spectral grandeur suggestive of Shakespeare.

The match was won, at least among my colleagues, and all agreed to act that night. The match! It was: "soon"; then, "in an hour"; then, "come and make up, it's time!"

One must never despair.

We had decided that if the hooting in the auditorium became too bad we would stop and one of us would recite Rimbaud's *Les Assis*, and another *La Grève des Forgerons*.

The crowded audience began laughing a full ten minutes before the rise of the curtain! They were going to be able to let themselves go to their hearts' content; for we were indeed all naked!

We proceeded simply and slowly. There were zones of silence lasting for more than twenty minutes on end. The critics were certainly less feverish than ninety-nine per cent. of the Deux Magots-ites.

The rise of the curtain was greeted by a formidable burst of laughter. We had none of the defences that speaking actors have recourse to at such times, such as lowering the voice so that those who want to hear will cry shsh. We simply had to perform.

The first ten minutes continued to be rowdy, but luckily my horse was upheld by the godlike wings of my celestial charwoman.

At the training of the horse silence fell. I felt it for the first time, congealing the audience, kneading it into a single dough. Holding both the audience and my horse by an imaginary bridle, I gave myself the luxury of improvising a bit. A scene, or number (call it what you will), at any rate it was theatre, that I ended with a gallop that shook the whole stage, the horse plunging, rearing, arching on its hind legs, and then a rapid exit at the gallop.

From this moment the audience was, if not mastered, at least acquiescent. I realised that those who had made fun of me the day before were at bottom true friends, and indeed they became my friends.

The rest of the performance passed off amid silence and interest, under the stupefied eyes of the watchmen, who didn't know what to make of it all. Hearing no noise on the stage and no noise in the auditorium they wondered if a performance was in progress at all or whether they hadn't better go home and get to bed.

But of course the mime did not consist solely of the horse. It was an epitome of all those means of expression that can possibly be presented by a *human being seen as an essential instrument of Dramatic Art*, to the almost total exclusion of the Word.

The expression of the body directly serving an action. Plastic exaltation pushed as far as gesture-symbol.

The only noise I allowed myself was the rhythm trodden on the boards by my bare feet, the wizard beating of my heart, and a whole poetry of breathing.

It was theatre in its primitive state.

For text: merely two brief explanatory scenes in cut-and-dry prose, and this was anyway a concession. And two long lyrical monologues said by the mother after she was dead.

The songs: two choirs of several voices without a valid text and for the most part murmured; in tune, thanks to a tuning-fork whose discreet note came to us from the wings.

We brought life to the elements. The torrid quivering Sun, Rain, a River, a Flood, Water, Drowning, Fire, a Conflagration, Birds (buzzards), Fish, a City, the Circulation of Traffic.

CHRISTIAN BÉRARD: costume for Mercure in *Amphitryon*

38

Dewey Dell, the girl, while picking cotton, made love, and immediately afterwards danced a dance of fecundity. She became pregnant under our eyes.

The mother went through a slow and painful agony which I translated, right up to the moment of death, by a long series of calculated breathings that made a ghastly effect, corresponding with the scrapings of the saw of the carpenter-son, who on his mother's instructions, was, during her agony, making her coffin.

The mother, when she had died and undergone brutal corpse-like rigidity, rose up in the most completely normal manner and wandered about the stage like a soul seeking its goal. She passed over into the world where reigns the Word.

Some time previously J. Copeau had been interviewed on the new trends of the theatre and had mentioned the words *romantic primitive*. The description seemed to me correct. In the return to the primitive state there was undoubtedly, if not romanticism, at least a lot of intellectualism.

After the performance the cast dispersed, well satisfied and borne away by friends. As for myself I found Artaud, whom I knew well already. The spectacle had put him into a state of exhilaration that was my immediate reward.

His fever was in accord with my own which had not yet abated, and we paced the Boulevard Clichy as if possessed.

Some days later he wrote the following about *Autour d'une Mère*:

There is, in J.-L. Barrault's play, a marvellous sort of centaur-horse, and great was our emotion on its appearance, as if J.-L. Barrault had brought magic into our lives.

This play is magical like those incantations of negro sorcerers when the tongue clicking against the palate brings rain to a whole countryside; or when the sorcerer, seeing a sick, wasted man, gives his breath the form of a strange discomfort and chases the sickness with his breath; in the same way in J.-L. Barrault's play a whole chorus of sounds spring into being at the moment of the mother's death.

D

I don't know whether this kind of success constitutes a masterpiece; but at any rate it is an event. When a transformation of atmosphere is such that a bristling audience is suddenly and blindly submerged and utterly disarmed, it should be recognised as an event.

There is a secret strength in this play that gains on the audience as a great love gains on a soul all set for rebellion.

A young and great love, a fresh vigour and a spontaneous lively effervescence flow through the disciplined movements and stylised mathematical gestures, like the twittering of birds through colonnades of trees in a magically laid-out forest. It is here, in this enchanted world, that Jean-Louis Barrault performs the antics of an untamed horse and that suddenly one is amazed to see him actually turn into a horse. His play brings home the irresistible significance of gesture; victoriously he demonstrates the importance of gesture and movement in space. He gives back to theatrical perspective a place it should never have lost. He fills the stage with pathos and with life.

It is on the stage and in relation to the stage that the whole spectacle is organised; it could only exist on the stage. And there is no point of scenic perspective but has its own moving significance.

In the animated gesticulations and discontinuous unfolding of figures there is a sort of direct physical appeal that the memory will not forget.

The memory will not forget the mother's death nor her cries belonging to both space and time, the epic crossing of the river, the fire rising in men's throats resembling, on the plane of gesture, another fire rising; and above all that man-horse running all through the piece, as if the very spirit of Fable had come down among us.

Up till now only the Théâtre Balinais seemed to have preserved a living trace of this lost spirit.

And if Jean-Louis Barrault has brought back the religious

spirit by using profane and descriptive means, what does it matter?—since all that is authentic is sacred, and his gestures are so lovely that they assume a symbolic significance. . . .

True, there are no symbols in Jean-Louis Barrault's play. And if criticism can be made of his gestures it would be that they give an illusion of symbolism when in fact they are dealing with reality; and it is thus that their action, violent and active though it be, has so to speak no prolongation.

It has no prolongation because it is merely descriptive, because it tells of external facts where souls have no place; it does not probe either thoughts or souls to the quick. And it is here, rather than in the question as to whether this form of theatre *is* theatre, that possible criticism lies.

The action has the means wherewith to make theatre; for theatre that lays before us a physical field demands that the field shall be filled, that the space shall be furnished with gestures, that the space shall be made to live magically and of itself, that an aviary of sound shall issue from it, that new relationships between sound, gesture and the human voice shall be discovered there; and we can truly say that that is the theatre such as J.-L. Barrault has made of it.

Yet such a realisation as his lacks the head-piece of the theatre, I mean the deep drama, the mystery that is deeper than the soul, the lacerating conflicts of the soul where gesture is but a means, where man is but a speck and where living people drink at their fountain-head. But who has ever drunk at the fountain-head of life?

It was at the *As I Lay Dying* period that I first made the acquaintance of Roger Blin, Jacques Prévert and the 'October Group' and that I first began to frequent the surréalists.

As I Lay Dying was my act of faith. I have never dared make it again.

What a lot of memories are associated with *As I Lay Dying*— some intimate and delicious, others pretty cockeyed, like the remark of someone in the audience repeated to me by my uncle some days later.

A man, after a minute or two, unable to contain himself any longer, leant towards his wife beside him and said: "If I had known it was so idiotic I would have brought the children." A comment, too, on education! Encouraging memories, like the extra matinée we gave at Louis Jouvet's request since he had heard of the play and wanted to see it but was acting every evening.

Gratitude to Jouvet for the interest he showed.

Some days later Dullin came to see it after all, and in the summer wrote a very affectionate article.

Now let us move on to more practical reflections.

It was owing to As I Lay Dying *that I made films.*

Marc Allegret had seen the play and kindly engaged me for a part in *Beaux Jours. It was owing to money earned in films that I was able to produce plays.*

Numantia ? Film money. *Hunger* ? Film money. And it was exclusively to money earned in cinema work that the Madeleine Renaud-Jean-Louis Barrault Company owed its birth.

Hence the theatre and the cinema always managed to supplement each other. And in work, too. The cinema, by forcing us to act as if we were under a microscope, recalls us to the sincerity and authenticity of the inner sensation. It brings home to us that we must not cheat.

Then along comes the theatre which urges us to exteriorise again, to play large and send far. It re-charges us as a battery is re-charged.

If in doing only film acting we run the risk of losing our diction (no voice, no diction), in doing only theatre we are in danger of letting ourselves slip, by intellectual sloth, into a craft composed of manners.

Yes, for the actor the theatre and the cinema complement each other. They are mutually beneficial.

JEAN HUGO: décor for *Antony and Cleopatra*

43

Professionally, artistically, socially, intellectually, indeed on all levels, the theatre and the cinema can be of assistance to each other.

When Raimu played *Le Bourgeois Gentilhomme*, didn't his films do their bit to help Molière to be appreciated? The admirer of Raimu, film star, went to see him act *Le Bourgeois Gentilhomme* and suddenly realised that this Molière was jolly different from the school one.

Merely on the plane of national education, Raimu, thanks to the cinema, beat the schoolmaster hands down.

There are countless actors who, as a result of their film reputation, have made people love Racine, Claudel, in fact the good theatre as a whole! And everyone knows that actors who have won a certain renown have a varying price in the cinema—just like on the Exchange or at the races.

I believe that a successful play, seen by only 20,000 people altogether, can considerably increase the film price of an actor just as if his success had been on the cinema and for millions of spectators.

These remarks are rather down-to-earth, I know, yet it seems to me useful to jot them down as they link up with an idea that never leaves me: *there exists to-day only one Art: Dramatic Art, and this comprises, at the moment, two main branches, the Theatre and the Cinema.* The Cinema and the Theatre, so narrowly complementary, should come to an ever closer understanding with each other, and form part of the same corporation.

Again, if it had not been for *As I Lay Dying*, which was first and foremost an avant-garde play, it would have taken me much longer to give of my best to the cinema; and if it had not been for the cinema I should never have been able to produce the plays I have produced.

I await the fusion of the two activities; both stand to gain by it.

5

The "Grenier des Augustins"

Living, to die, and dying, to live.
HERACLITUS

July 26, 1935.

MY DEAR BARRAULT,
  You absolutely must let me know the answer to these two questions by return of post.

When will you be back in Paris?

Do you seriously intend to return to the Atelier for the forthcoming season?

As soon as I hear from you I shall write and tell you my plans.

In haste, and with best wishes,

CHARLES DULLIN.

This was the letter Charles Dullin wrote me in the summer.[1]

I took the plunge and left the Atelier. Freely, yet against my will.

I have always had to fight against my timorous nature; hence I have often, by an act of will and against my nature, put myself in situations where I have jolly well had to sink or swim.

It was in the same frame of mind that I subsequently left the Comédie Française which I loved so dearly.

The method seems to me excellent so long as one's reflexes are sound and one is prepared to swim.

Yet the Atelier had made me so much its own that for some months I wondered whether I would ever act again. I saw the theatre in and through Charles Dullin and could not conceive of it otherwise.

[1] This letter has always seemed to me profoundly human. Left to myself, I should never have dared to leave the Atelier. This letter gave me a handle. Did Charles Dullin write it, I wonder, with the delicate intention of helping me?

It was Salacrou who brought me back to the surface by practically *forcing* me to act in *Un Homme comme les Autres*; and even then I could only stand sixty performances.

Professionally I was dangerously exacting—dangerously, for myself!

Thus I walked down from Montmartre with a heavy heart, an uncaptained soul, drifting, anguished, and I rented an attic in the Rue des Grands Augustins. A magnificent spot that has since become still more magnificent—Picasso's studio. Jean Dasté, I and other colleagues of *As I Lay Dying* formed an embryonic company called: Le Grenier des Augustins.

I should say at once that the "Grenier des Augustins" did almost nothing. I captained the ship badly. Jean Dasté, quite rightly, lost heart and went off. But the life we led there was outstanding for its freedom, variety, fantasticness and high spirits.

The Grenier years consisted solely of Life. No work was done, but it was a very enriching experience.

The October Group—Prévert, Desnos, and above all Breton and G. Bataille; the celebrations of the death of Louis XVI; the surrealist manifestos; Itkine; the scarlet Devil; Wednesdays, when everyone came for a picnic meal; the reading of plays by the tragic light of candles; Gilles Margaritis who was preparing his 'cello number and found his little harmonium at the Grenier; the nights spent with the Cuban composers; the revolutionary debates; the ever-open door; beds in every corner; the moneylessness; and always a kindly atmosphere that never lacked humour; the daily dropping-in of Antonin Artaud. Taken all together, those higgledy-piggledy things were extremely instructive.

Here is an anecdote which may perhaps give an idea of the Grenier atmosphere.

I said that every Wednesday there was a picnic meal. First only friends came, by invitation. Then those friends brought their friends. Then it was open house to everyone. The friends' friends brought along other friends. Then the original friends got bored

with seeing so many people and stopped coming. At the end
hardly anyone knew who anyone was. So much so that one day
in the Rue de Rennes a man walking past me smiled. I smiled
back but rather uncertainly. He stopped, retraced his steps:
"Don't you remember me?" he said. "I must admit . . ." And
he went on: "But we dined together last Wednesday at
Barrault's!"

I never found out whom he had taken for Barrault.

That anarchist existence had its nobility, and the royal representative of this anarchist nobility was undeniably Antonin
Artaud.

6

Antonin Artaud

*I know that I am pleasing to those
whom I specially need to please.*

ANTIGONE

AFTER the strong personality of Charles Dullin and the exacting (yes, as exacting as Alceste) friendship of Étienne Decroux, I have been most impressed by the grandiose character of Antonin Artaud.

I had 'undergone' Charles Dullin to the point of resembling him. And I was to undergo Artaud in the same way, but to the point of resembling him exactly.

Indeed Artaud was vastly amused when I gave him imitations of himself; and I remember one day, when I had done one of my imitations, he ran out of the room in a frenzy and shouted along the streets: "I've been robbed of my personality, I've been robbed of my personality!" I didn't see him again for three days. But when we finally found each other we laughed heartily about it.

For in his most feverishly excited moments, Artaud almost always kept a reserve of prodigious lucidity. Artaud could always protect himself by his uncanny capacity for humour.

In his most embittered snarl Artaud could keep a flicker of a smile near the very corner of his mouth by which his intimates were not deceived.

Artaud, no doubt dissatisfied with the artificial joys provided by the stage, carried his own theatrical ability into life. He genuinely loved the part he played, and he and it wore themselves out together. He became theatre. His life is precisely a tragedy.

He had an extraordinary forehead that he always thrust in front of him as if to light his path. From this magnificent brow sheaves

48

of hair sprouted. His piercing blue eyes sank into their sockets as if in that way they could scrutinise further. The eyes of a rapacious bird—an eagle. His thin pinched nose quivered incessantly.

His mouth, like the whole of Artaud, preyed upon itself. His spine was bent like a bow. His lean arms with their long hands, like two twisted forked trunks, seemed to be trying to plough up his belly.

His voice, rising up from his innermost caverns, bounded towards his head with such rare force that it was dashed against the sounding board of his forehead. It was both sonorous and hollow, strong yet immediately muted. He was essentially an aristocrat. Artaud was a prince.

His thoughts were luminous and like lightning. He was a creature of fire, Prometheus' own child.

Tantrist *Yoga*, the Egyptian *Book of the Dead*, the *Upanishad*, the *Golden Verses* of Pythagoras—those were the books he gave me to read. He detested narcotics and always said the worst things about them. He never wanted me to touch them.

He had a double personality. The first was dizzily lucid and had the most joyful wit. It was aware of everything in a permanent and even an alarming way. Aware of everything that was happening all around—to right, to left, in front, behind, very near, very far away. He took in the Present in all its meanings with all his senses. The perceptions of a fly.

The other Artaud was a smouldering creature, a seer. One had the impression that a touring car had been fitted with the engine of an aeroplane. Without sedatives Artaud exploded on all sides. He was royally beautiful.

He was an engrossing man. Obviously I devoured *Le Théâtre et la Peste*, *Le Théâtre de la Cruauté*, together with the other articles that the N.R.F. had just assembled and published under the title of *Le Théâtre et son Double*. *Le Théâtre et son Double* is far and away the most important thing that has been written about the theatre in the twentieth century.

There are five works that I always and unhesitatingly recommend to young actors. Five works that are mutually complementary and form their own five-point star.

Aristotle's *Poetica*   *Les Trois Discours* de Corneille
Le Préface de Cromwell (V. Hugo)   *The Art of the Theatre* (Gordon
                    Le Théâtre et son Double (Artaud)   Craig)

Le Théâtre et son Double should be read and read again.

Artaud oozed magical desires. He was the metaphysician of the theatre.

I often saw him landing at the Grenier with two or three roses in his hand, which he was bringing for me. But in the course of our long nocturnal conversations together he gave me, with equal grace and generosity, some of his secrets, some of his clues.

The confidences I had made him about the PERMANENT SILENCE that haunted me and about the continuous perception of the PRESENT that I longed to seize hold of encouraged him to tell me about some of his own discoveries.

Artaud was a poet first and foremost. He was a wonderful writer, as everyone knows; but he was also an actor. And it was in the character of a poet that he always played.

He had played with Dullin in the early days of the Atelier. One day, while rehearsing a play Dullin was producing in which Artaud was supposed to be taking the part of the Emperor Charlemagne, Artaud was suddenly seen to approach the throne on all fours. Dullin feared Artaud and was on guard against his reactions. Yet this ascent to the throne on all fours seemed to him . . . a bit too . . . stylised. So it was with great caution that Dullin set about dissuading Artaud from his interpretation and inducing him to agree to a more likely stylisation. But suddenly Artaud reared up, erect, and brandishing his arm imperiously cried: "Oh, if it's Realism you're after! Well then!!"

Artaud turned his attention with no less sagacity to the problem of diction and the importance of gesture. But he was unable to broach a subject except as an alchemist, a magician. And that spirit of alchemy found echoes in myself.

There follow some notes that may serve as a LITTLE TREATISE ON THE ALCHEMY OF THE THEATRE, on the supposition that such a treatise may be of interest. And by now I am a bit vague as to Artaud's share in these notes.

AN ATTEMPT AT A LITTLE TREATISE
ON THE ALCHEMY OF THE THEATRE

Oh, mes parents, que je vous en veux.
LE BOURGEOIS GENTILHOMME

DICTION

A. *Vowels*

In writing there are five vowels, A, E, I, O, U. In speech there are fifteen. For each of the five written ones:

> the same vowel open,
> the same vowel half-open,
> the same vowel closed.

But the voice makes use of four times fifteen. Each of the fifteen forms of the speech vowels is placed either:

> on the bottom lip,
> or in the throat,
> or on the roof of the mouth,
> or on the upper lip.

the bottom lip corresponds with the digestive centre,
the throat corresponds with the sensual centre,
the roof of the mouth corresponds with the intellectual centre,
the upper lip corresponds with the nervous centre.

It is the greater or less rapidity of the frequency of the vibrations of the diaphragm which causes the vowel to knock either on the bottom lip, the throat, the roof of the mouth, or the upper lip.

The vowel is a blow of the breath which becomes a sound by its vibrations.

We read in the *Book of the Dead* that the initiated have to present themselves before the gods at the judgment with their voices correctly pitched. The exercise for pitching the voice correctly consists in enunciating the consonance "OM."

To begin with the diaphragm has to vibrate slowly, then more and more quickly, and by an abdominal contraction which intensifies the frequency of the vibration, the vowel O is projected into the air and strikes the extremity of the roof of the mouth, just behind the top teeth.

The gentle closing of the lips moulds the consonant M and at the same time produces the vibration in the whole head which resounds OM.

With the cycle of the four principal positions of the voice playing on the fifteen spoken vowels a whole series of exercises like scales can be constructed. Thus the vowel is a sort of flake of sound that issues from the breath: an invention that has its birth in man's breath: an essential manifestation of his life: a proof in sound that he is breathing.

B. *The Consonant*

The consonant is the result of a muscular contraction. The consonant is a plastic invention—like the cut of a chisel. The muscles of the mouth contract at the passing of the breath-vowel they have fashioned. And they enrich it with a consonant.

C. *The Syllable*

The syllable, made up of a consonant and a vowel, is thus the outcome of a breath and a gesture (of the mouth, in this case).

N.B.—Hence there is no essential difference between proper bodily expression (itself made up of muscular contractions and breathings which are muscular too), and the WORD, that is to say Speech. On condition that speech should be regarded as the most skilled physical expression of which the HUMAN BEING is capable.

It was the memory of these considerations that later helped me to appreciate Claudel's use of speech and to love his definition of

the Word as "an intelligible mouthful". Speech is quite simply
a plastic exercise of the mouth. It is similar, in kind, to the gesture,
which is, so to speak, a plastic exercise of the body. Speech and
Gesture are not like pear and apple, dog and cat, but one and the
same fruit, like a garden peach and a wild peach.

D. *Breathing*

Just breathing alone provides a whole laboratory of magic.

It is Breathing that maintains the life of man. In man's
unchanging permanent state, and particularly when he is asleep,
he is animated by what is called unconscious breathing.

Hence his first great temptation is to try to become conscious
of his unconscious breathing, and this is an extremely difficult
task. As soon as awareness of breathing occurs we cannot help
modifying our breathing which thereupon ceases to be unconscious. It is an exercise that quickly tires the nervous system. Only
extremely well-balanced people are capable—at least they tell
me they are—of becoming conscious of their breathing without
altering it. Hence unconscious breathing and conscious breathing
have a very narrow line of demarcation; they easily become
confused. And then follows the second great temptation: by
exercises in conscious breathing to try to attain to the unconscious,
and thence plumb the soul and its states and try to modify them.

The Two Kinds of Conscious Breathing

There are two kinds of breathing. We will call the one FIRST
breathing and the other SECOND breathing.

The FIRST serves life's purpose, and we should never make use
of it in the theatre.

Only the SECOND should be used—and by this means we
shall never lose our breath.

Method for using SECOND Breathing

The whole secret of breathing lies in breathing-out. Never
mind about breathing-in. (And that goes for the figurative sense,
too, the moral sense: never mind about in-spiration, only about

a-spiration. "I can love only those who groan in their search", Pascal said.)

By a muscular dilation of the thoracic cage and a depression of the diaphragm, the air comes in.

Swallow so as to assure the decontraction of the pharynx while breathing out.

Then breathe-out slowly using only the diaphragm (which is anyway the most sensitive part of the muscular apparatus of breathing and solely responsible for the *diminuendo* and *pianissimo,* which are the very art of diction), but maintain the rest of the thoracic cage as dilated as possible as if the tips of the breasts were straining upward and forward. When the diaphragm is completely restocked like the piston of a syringe and you think you have no breath left, you have still used only the theatre breathing, namely the second breathing.

Let everything go and you will see that you still have more breath, but it is the breath of the first breathing, the *breath of the actor.*

Second breathing being the *breath of your part.* ("Is it surprising that in the midst of all these considerations I find it so difficult to act! ! !")

When you act you are two people, the *actor* and his *part,* so it is perfectly normal to have two breathings. The first for the actor, to keep him alive, the second for his part—the breathing of the diaphragm, the sensitive breathing. What follows has to do solely with second breathing.

Respiratory Solfeggio

By suitable exercise in breathing the unconscious can be attained and the actor can be orientated towards a desired state.

The Ternary

Whether it be question of the body, the soul and the mind; sensibility, sentiment and consent; instinct, understanding and intelligence; the earth, the moon and the sun; purity, virtue and truth; passive, neuter and active; whether it be question of the

CHRISTIAN BÉRARD: costume-sketch for *Les Fourberies de Scapin*

Cabalistic ternary or the Holy Trinity, we have recognised since the time of Pythagoras the permanent existence of the ternary.

Masculine—feminine—neuter.

Every ternary has six principal components which are:

>masculine—feminine—neuter
>masculine—neuter—feminine
>feminine—masculine—neuter
>feminine—neuter—masculine
>neuter—masculine—feminine
>neuter—feminine—masculine.

Applied to breathing the three elements of the Ternary are:

>out-breathing—in-breathing—retention.

And if we recognise the existence in life of the WILL—whether it comes from the self, black will issuing from the self, or whether it be imposed—we can amuse ourselves by indefinitely composing breathing combinations that will finally put us in a given state of soul. A thorough-going *solfeggio of breathing*.

Which is an art in itself.

A comparison with Painting will help us to understand this better. Painting comprises three basic colours. Another ternary, BLUE—RED—YELLOW, in which each corresponds to a colour so-called complementary made up of the two others:

>RED and its complementary BLUE-YELLOW or GREEN;
>BLUE and its complementary RED-YELLOW or ORANGE;
>YELLOW and its complementary BLUE-RED or PURPLE.

To the ternary, to its six principal components and to the different combinations brought to the ternary by the complementaries, two influences must be added, whether BLACK or WHITE. It is the intervention of these two influences, BLACK and WHITE, that causes the number of combinations deriving from this ternary to be unlimited, the number of 'broken tones' to be unlimited.

That is the very art of Painting.

E

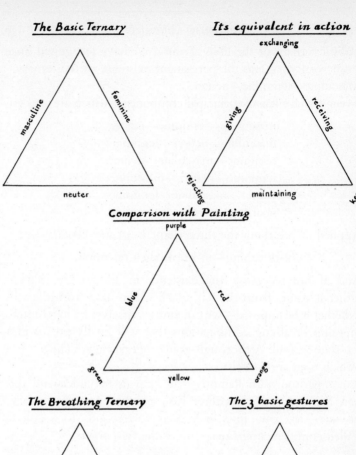

The Basic Ternary

exchanging

masculine *feminine*

neuter

Its equivalent in action

giving *receiving*

rejecting *maintaining* *keeping*

Comparison with Painting

purple

blue *red*

green *yellow* *orange*

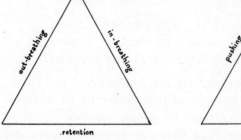

The Breathing Ternary

out-breathing *in-breathing*

retention

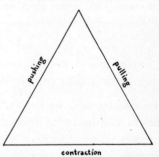

The 3 basic gestures

pushing *pulling*

contraction

The two influences :   BLACK - interior will imposed on space
WHITE - external will imposed from without

58

The art of breathing, like the art of gesture, starts out from these two data: (i) the breathing ternary and (ii) the white or black influences of the external or internal will, and if it is not more complete than the art of painting, it is equally so.

masculine—feminine—neuter

equals: out-breathing—in-breathing—retention (for breathing)
equals: pushing—pulling—contraction (for gesture) and all that is equivalent to:

giving—receiving—maintaining;

giving-receiving = exchanging (which is the complementary of maintaining)

receiving-maintaining = keeping (which is the complementary of giving)

giving-maintaining = rejecting (which is the complementary of receiving).

The combinations that could be made with the help of this ternary, of its principal components and of the complementary combinations, would be limited if no other influences came into play; whether the influence that the Self tries to impose on the external world = BLACK FORCE, or the influence that the external world imposes on the self = WHITE FORCE.

Let us take an example:

My out-breathing is *imposed*, that is to say that an influence external to my own will imposes this out-breathing upon me. Immediately I summon up my will to take in more air, to breathe-in, and I retain the air as long as I can in my lungs. But faced with this external influence my will is weak and I can't postpone my out-breathing; hence I distort my breathing.

Imposed out-breathing; willed in-breathing and retention. That is a breathing of weakness and inferiority, such as occurs in sickness.

Take the opposite: when my in-breathing is imposed, as when I am startled. If this imposed in-breathing is caused by an unpleasant surprise, as in fear, then I immediately summon up my will and breathe-out as hard as I can and shut up. But fresh in-breathing is imposed on me from without, and so on. That is FEAR.

Imposed in-breathing, voluntary out-breathing, voluntary retention.

If on the other hand the imposed in-breathing were caused by something pleasurable, I would summon up my will to hold it and the combination would be:

Imposed in-breathing, voluntary retention, and—if my pleasure is of short duration—voluntary out-breathing; if I am not strong enough to sustain the delight—imposed out-breathing. A state corresponding to JOY.

The combinations are infinite.

As for knowing how all this helps us to act, that is quite another matter.

At all events this is unquestionably the basis of a solfeggio which, if fixed, could develop both breathing power and the plastic faculties of the body.

This solfeggio is as valid for the art of the theatre as real solfeggio is valid for music.

We have seen in passing that, parallel with our breathing solfeggio, there could be a solfeggio for the body. I use the word *solfeggio* deliberately so as to bring home that these considerations and exercises are of value exclusively for training purposes. They are the starting-point of a thorough-going technical training. And it is more worth-while doing exercises for the development and agility of the body than endlessly massacring Racine's alexandrines or Corneille's verses. At any rate, as Paul Valéry said: "Dabbling in what one doesn't know by means of what one does is divine!"

*

If anyone had asked me at that time what the theatre was, I should have given my usual answer: "The theatre is the art of the Human Being," and I should have added, "in space."

After having been so struck by the Silence upon which Life reposes, and then by the forward-progress of Life being made up of a countless number of *successive Presents*, I was quite bowled over by the conflict between the opposing Wills of the Human Being and his Space.

The External World and the Self.

The external will is either in harmony or discord with my own will. Impossible henceforth to isolate man from his space. In Man face-to-face with his Space lies the basis of theatre.

It is remarkable that all art is the outcome of one element confronting another. It is the song that springs from the friction of two elements.

> A brush rubs canvas;
>
> A pen scrapes paper;
>
> A bodkin scratches a metal plate;
>
> A chisel chips stone;
>
> A bow rubs catgut;
>
> A hammer strikes a string, and so on.

In the theatre: a Human Being struggles in space. And what song springs up? A life seen not especially from the angle of its colours, nor from the angle of its shapes, nor yet from the angle of its sounds, but essentially from the angle of its Presence in motion, that is to say its *Exchanges*, its *Movements properly so called*, and its underlying *Rhythm*. Life in its *Becoming*. Life seized on the point of a needle between a Present that is passing and a Present that is coming. And on this so fine edge the infinite simultaneity of all the conflicts in Presence. Exchanges, harmonies, enmities, attractions, refusals, pretences, observations, settling of accounts.

And if I had been asked whether the Human Being, in Space, was the one element capable of giving birth to this song of Life, of Life seen from the angle of *Exchange*, of *Movement* and of *Rhythm*, I should have answered that the Human Being alone was the appropriate element, for he alone can unite, in the *Present* and *simultaneously*:

a palpitating breathing—Seat of Exchanges,

a spinal column, Seat of Movement,

a heart whose beating is at the very basis of rhythm—systole, diastole, short beat, long beat, the iambic foot.

I should have said, too, that I no longer saw the difference between bodily expression properly so-called or the *art of gesture*, and the delicate mechanism of the mouth which creates the word, or the *art of Speech*. I should have added that I believed in a marriage of these two possible forms of expression deriving from the same origin, and that I had come to see the possibility of passing from the one to the other, from Gesture to Speech, the one upheld by the other, the one in harmony with the other, the one in association with the other.

And then I came to feel the need for TOTAL THEATRE.

CONCERNING TOTAL THEATRE

A Concerto for Man

Starting out from the Human Being seen in Space, from the Human Being seen as the essential instrument of dramatic art, it is possible to conceive of a concerto for Man being written one day.

As Man is an instrument, why has no one ever written a concerto for him?—like a concerto for the piano, the violin, the organ, or the saxophone?

If such a work were attempted, how would it pan out?

Let us imagine tiers of seats mounting in a semicircle; in the centre something like half an arena.

The seats are occupied by the orchestra. On the extreme right of the semicircle stands the conductor. On the extreme left the choir of human beings, for it is correct that the instrument—the human being—should also be represented in the orchestra.

A man enters the arena.

The concerto readily becomes man's problem in space, man's problem in the universe.

The omnipresence of the orchestra; the infinity of propositions; some are taken up by the man, others are suggested; in their turn they are taken up or rejected by the orchestra.

Chords—harmonies—discords—dissensions, and so on.

Gesture carried to the extreme limit of its capacity. As well as—

> breath,
> cries,
> articulation,
> SPEECH, in fact.

Perhaps one day a dramatic poet will be tempted by such a subject.

*

Artaud had gone off to Mexico some time before. I felt a ferocious need to 'objectivise' myself (as Laforgue puts it). The engine was packing up under the strain of these diabolical flights into the abstract; I had to get into gear.

It was then that André Masson, just back from Spain, spoke to me about a tragedy by Cervantes: *Numantia*.

Adrienne Monnier lent me an old translation of it. Avidly I threw myself upon *Numantia*.

7

Numantia

IN 1937, *Numantia.*
Exactly two years had passed since *As I Lay Dying.*
Two years in which I made films, enthused ecstatically in a vacuum, and acquired scattered information.

Both from the professional point of view and from the point of view of my personal life I felt the need to settle down.

Numantia was a classic, but sufficiently removed from the French classical spirit to give me an opportunity to prove myself without taking too great a risk.

Numantia had tragic grandeur and human nobility.

Numantia, a free city besieged by Scipio Africanus, was, alas, a topical theme.

"Numantia Liberty!"

The *Numantia* venture helped me to rediscover the human heart.

Numantia came just in time to de-intellectualise me, to make me a man again. Man as a 'volitive unity' as Pythagoras says.

It was *Numantia* that lifted me from the nursery garden where I had been growing and replanted me in the wide open air. And at the same time a parallel process was occurring in my personal life. It was at the *Numantia* period that my life as a man began.

Numantia was my first production. In *As I Lay Dying* I had transposed a novel into a mime and had thus by-passed the problem of production. That had been an author's work, a special kind of author's work.

With *Numantia* I had to orchestrate a real theatrical subject and, what's more, a tragedy. To this work I had to bring the knowledge I had already acquired and put it at the service, if not

JEAN HUGO: décor for *Phèdre*

of a great piece of writing, at least of an exclusively theatrical theme.

Hard facts: The *As I Lay Dying* venture cost me my inheritance from my father, that is to say about 12,000 francs; *Numantia* cost me what I had been able to save from my film earnings: rather more than 40,000 francs.

To start with I nearly hired a charming little theatre in the Rue Saint-Martin called, I think, the Comédie Saint-Martin. The rent would have been 20,000 francs a year, but I was daunted by all the other expenses. I don't know what has become of this theatre; it was a true theatre, like the Montmartre Theatre, or the Grenelle where Artaud had produced plays in the past when it was called the Alfred Jarry.

Anyhow it seemed to me that the material outlay would be less if I simply hired the famous Antoine Theatre from Monsieur Paston.

So it was at the Antoine that *Numantia* was put on.

If I took several parts it was because I couldn't find anyone else to play them. My ambition spurred me to try to induce Dalio to play the Magician, for I had a great admiration for his talent, but Dalio wasn't free. I have always had a predilection for great actors.

The décor and costumes were done by André Masson, who had become a close friend.

For noises off and musical accompaniment a young French Cuban, Carpentier, helped me, as well as Charles Wolff, who owned a wonderful library of records.

Charles Wolff was to die from torture at the hands of the Germans in the early days of the Occupation. What has become of his magnificent collection of records, I wonder?

I unearthed my Romans from a gymnastic club at Aubervilliers and the six boys I engaged gave me great satisfaction.

A large part of the *As I Lay Dying* group made up my cast.

Roger Blin, Georges Rollin, Stéphane Audel, Cariel and J. Berthier joined us. The work was enthralling and taxing.

If, in putting on a show, one had only to cope with the work of rehearsals and the technical side of the play, the task would be within the bounds of human possibility. But what makes the whole enterprise so exhausting is the influx of difficulties that arise quite outside the work proper.

For the first time in my life I was a manager. I was 'doing business' with a Paris theatre manager. I got to know, to my cost, about special privileges, about all the servile obligations of the theatre, and even about the places reserved for 'paid clappers' (though I think this custom has at last disappeared). I learnt the ritual of curtain-calls, the expected return from programmes, the bar, the cloakroom. I heard tell of people who bought tickets and then resold them at a profit. In fact I got to know about a whole section of the life of the theatre of which I had been ignorant up till then, a number of people who batten on the theatre without apparently contributing anything to it.

I am well aware that there have been constant attempts to put an end to personal publicity, tips for the attendants, tips in the cloakroom, and the whole spirit that uses every nook and cranny of the theatre for financial profit; but I also know that all attempts made along these lines have failed. As if one moved heaven and earth to bale out a leaking boat while forgetting to find out the cause of the leak.

I discovered, too, as I have done often, oh, how often, since, that a theatrical undertaking is an industry.

I know too that the method of subsidies can never bring a profession prosperity and that a real profession must be capable of living on its own resources.

But on the other hand I know that in certain theatres it is only the revenue accruing from 'concessions' (personal publicity, window-dressing, soft drinks, programmes, cloakroom and the other little activities more or less on the side) that enables the director to live until finally he is no longer interested in anything but the exploitation of these things and ceases in an alarming way to be interested in what is going on on the stage.

Everything that happens in the building of a theatre is tricky and exciting.

The theatre is a place of oblivion. The Japanese call actors "dispensers of oblivion". The spectator who goes to the theatre should feel, from the moment he crosses the threshold, indeed while still on the pavement outside, an atmosphere prepared for the dispensing of OBLIVION.

When the spectator enters the theatre he should be treated as if he were entering a luxurious baths establishment, but psychical baths. He has come to take a *bath of oblivion*. If, on entering, he feels that he is being treated as if he were in the post office or the dairy, he becomes disenchanted, and his disillusion puts him in a bad temper and he becomes peevish.

Obviously if the theatre is to live the spectator must pay for his seat. Yet I am sure he would like to get the impression of being welcomed by friends.

I dare say that there are further simple refinements to be found which would be appreciated by the spectator.

Naturally he would soon get used to these refinements and feel a need for others. So the theatre must think of other nice things to offer. After all that is all we do in life when we want to give pleasure.

And what is the theatre if not a vehicle of Joy? It is joy that we seek, *joy*, the goal of our ascent! The joy of feeling that we are alive after all our sufferings, of feeling that we have been on the nerve of life.

Very well, this ascent towards Joy must start on the pavement, at the very moment of entering the theatre, when we lean our elbows on the box-office ledge.

So it was being torn between my first anxieties as a manager and the effort of rehearsal work that made my labours so exhausting.

It is only with time that we learn to reconcile these two contradictory activities. It is only with time that we become a Jack-of-all-trades: "Do you want to speak to the coachman, sir, or the cook?" and that we can cope with being pulled in all directions.

The function of a producer is a much more complicated craft than is imagined.

The production of a play does not involve the directly artistic side only; it involves the management of everything touching on the artistic side.

Producing a play does not lie only in making others act, nor in agreeing to or turning down the suggestions of the designer or musician. No; we must also be competent to replace others, to make designs for the designer, to set the musician on the right lines; and we do not attain the full liberty of a producer unless we can measure the décor to a nicety, direct the head mechanic, rebut the tortuous answers of the head electrician, the chief upholsterer, the head property-man, the stage manager and the stage director. Even in the best run houses the workmen, nine times out of ten from a sort of qualm of conscience, slip out of our grasp and we have to force them to do what we want. So we have to know experimentally what we do want, and that involves a detailed and craftsman's knowledge of the means at our disposal.

And that is not all. Before attaining the full liberty of a producer we must know how to make the necessary overtures to the Authors' Society, know the price and quality of materials, understand the workings of the box-office, supervise the arrangement of the auditorium on a first night, know how to read the plan of the auditorium and the tally of the receipts, understand how the dresses are kept in good repair, know how many hours are required for the changing of a play (hours for the staff). It is only then that we have won the right to sit in the stalls and watch others work and try to make them better even than they are.

We must resemble those factory directors who have gone through all the occupations of which their factory is made up and who, thanks to this rung-by-rung climb, cannot be fooled by their foremen; not those who come from a so-called top, a theoretical top, and who in fact have no right to direct the work of others nor make money from the work of others.

At the *Numantia* period I knew nothing about all this. But in any case I delighted in my sufferings. I revelled in my young life as a producer and I acted the life as much as I lived it.

My furies were olympian. My indignations were extreme. I gave myself, exhausted myself, wore myself out here, there and everywhere. It was exquisite, an orgy of anxieties.

The costumes were delivered only on the day of the dress-rehearsal: we skirted catastrophe—marvellous! I had practically lost my voice; it was tragic, but heroic. I was 6,000 francs short to meet the bill for the costumes. It was a disgrace, but a martyrdom!

And that won me a demonstration of the truest friendship from Desnos. He was there when the costumes arrived and when he saw that I had no money left he slipped away from the theatre and fetched from the T.S.F. where he worked his month's salary in advance which he pressed into my hand, to get "us" out of our jam, he said. Six thousand francs! his salary for a whole month.

Dear Desnos! I was talking just now about the Joy of life. Desnos had the keenest joy in life of any man I know. He was so happy just to be alive on the earth. He shared the lives of his fellow-creatures with such zest. He had such a sense of true friendship. He relished life as no one else, its good times with its hard times, its riches with its kicks, nights spent in fevered conversation, jazz and drink, and also long intoxicating salutary tramps in the woods, bathing "in streams cold as a razor's edge," "oh heart of a bumpkin and guts of a lion!" "let's piss in the clover and spit in the vetch."

What a rich nature! which he lavished out of love for love, out of the greatest Love for love. Desnos, a true friend. Desnos' whole life was inspired by an absolute generosity. Desnos died a deportee, having upheld the morale of his comrades. Desnos will never cease to accompany me and be beside me to help me in my conduct through life.

Numantia was a success. I had rented the Antoine for a fortnight. There had to be special police for the last performances. We ought perhaps to have given more performances but the theatre was already booked by Alibert who was awaiting our departure to put on a new Marseilles musical. In any case our joy had been satisfied, we had laboured, we had acted, lived the venture, and exhibited our work; and already certain things in the play displeased me and I was not sorry to stop. Always insatiable, always dissatisfied.

On the professional plane I was faulty. We must act for it is our fate. I learnt that later. At the time I was a little too new in the profession.

At the final performance we were glad and sad. Glad of the result, sad to feel that a slice of our life was becoming the past, in other words dead. The work had made such a mark on us that when we separated in the street we were still acting the play.

We had again given ourselves utterly. That was good.

From the technical point of view, what are the fruitful memories of *Numantia*?

The décor. Happy arrangement thanks to the wall that opened and shut solely by the will of the characters. Machinery belonging essentially to the drama. Nothing in excess and what there was dramatically telling.

Costumes. Masson had shown himself to be a true theatre man. Design and colour of the costumes essentially dramatic.

Numantia is a collective play. By the different values playing on each other Masson gave the impression of numbers. The masks corresponded exactly to the symbols; the attributes were correct. The bull's head, *Numantia's* emblem, had the desired tragic grandeur.

Groupings. The groupings which I arranged for the first time myself were successful.

The Roman soldiers. Stylisation of a collective gesture to suit a collective character. I had given the Roman soldiers not an individual gesticulation but something chosen from the collective gestures of a troop on the march and in this way the six of them gave the impression of a whole company.

The value of these gestures. Nothing is more satisfying to me than those discoveries that bear no direct resemblance to the object, which become isolated objects with their own life, yet express the object more exactly than the object itself.

Numantia was my first production.

Thanks to its success I had my reward. Claudel had been an eager spectator. Every evening a box was reserved for him and he brought his friends along. Darius Milhaud, who has always shown me such adorable affection, introduced us and I called on Claudel some days later in his flat in the Rue Jean Goujon. A brief but exhilarating encounter.

With *Numantia* I closed my sixth theatrical year. I was not behind-hand from the all-round point of view of artistic forma-tion. But I was behind on the technical side and particularly with regard to the current technique of the actor.

My voice had not yet found its pitch. My acting was nervous, taut, cramped. I could not apply all my lovely theories. I was hardly an actor at all. A pupil in his second year at the Con-servatoire, whom I should have despised some years before, was ten times more skilful than myself.

I came out of *Numantia* with a redoubled desire to learn, this time, the straightforward profession of an actor, to learn without thinking overmuch, to learn by means of the daily infiltration of acting.

I had before my eyes the outstanding example of Madeleine Renaud who seemed to me more and more to be the prototype of the professional actor. What a pity that convention disqualifies me from talking about Her![1]

I decided, then, to accept everything without too much reflection, and it was thus the following season I leapt at the opportunity given me by Alice Cocéa to play the *Misanthrope* opposite her.

[1] She is the author's wife.

For three months I floundered among Alceste's 900 lines, which earned me an additional excommunication from Decroux and a sharp rebuke from Jouvet. But this kind of cold shower knocked off my corners and my star guided me well; it put on my path the man who could at that moment do me the most good. I formed a close friendship with Charles Granval.

8

Charles Granval

AFTER Dullin and Artaud it was Granval who made the deepest mark on me—but with the reserve without which he couldn't live.

Dullin	Artaud	Granval
EARTH	SUN	MOON
Birth	Trial by fire	Sentiment
The body	The mind	The soul
Purity	Truth	Virtue
The pioneer	The prophet	The artist

Granval belonged to a third generation of actors.

He was born in the Théâtre Français at Rouen, of which his father, an actor and son of an actor, was manager. Thus Granval was what is called his father's child.

Granval was a man of the avant-garde. I went to the Théâtre Français as a schoolboy (when, without having been warned for or against, I laughed till I cried because A. Lambert and Madeleine Roch struck me as being so funny in *Hernani*), but the only play that really impressed me there was *A quoi rêvent les Jeunes Filles* with a décor by Marie Laurencin and music taken from Debussy. And it was Granval who had put it on. That must have been in 1924–1925.

But the play which caused a minor revolution in Paris was *Les Fourberies de Scapin* put on by Granval in 1921.

When we left the Comédie Française in 1946, *A quoi rêvent les Jeunes Filles* and the *Fourberies de Scapin* were being played, and still in Granval's production. How many productions hold good for twenty-five years?

74

Granval was a true artist of the avant-garde, yes, but his anarchy was not bitter. He was too much of an artist to be fanatical. He lacked the shortcomings that go to the make-up of aggressive natures.

Third generation of actors, I said. A greenhouse flower is a brittle flower: early broken, early bruised, soon discouraged. And moreover Granval had against him the very thing that gave him his superiority: a more or less complete culture.

At the Conservatoire he had studied under Leloir; he took his first prize in *Fortunio*, I think, and as far as I know entered the Comédie Française in 1902.

Granval would never have told me those details about himself; it is not from him that I know them, which is why I have so few facts. Granval would never have allowed me to talk about him although I think this writing I am doing would please him. He would never have undertaken a book like this—he would have found it pedantic and pretentious as well as tiring and irksome.

Granval was a *pensionnaire* for eighteen years. When he retired in 1935 after thirty-three years of the Théâtre Français, during which he produced fifty-five plays, he was not even a top-ranking partner.

He called the Français "the central pharmacy" but he loved it too much to be able to leave it.

Since that time I too have got to know something about our classics and have glimpsed at the deep knowledge that the ancestral repertoire of the Français brings to whoever wants it; and I can appreciate the problems of choice that must arise for anyone with avant-garde preoccupations. The rough and raw avant-garde man, the sort that rates knowledge low, can easily get his effects. The problem is to remain on terms with knowledge. Granval's capacity for initiative was held in check by all the knowledge he had acquired at the Français, for it deprived him, in his own eyes, of the right to make mistakes.

An ignorant man can afford to step out and if he has the temperament he can make innovations. But a man with a cultured temperament is cautious about embarking on new things, for in innovation there lies the risk of error—a risk about which culture can make one too wary; moreover to an over-artistic temperament such as Granval's, error seems a lapse in taste, and mere fear of lacking taste would deter him from the chanciness of innovation.

And yet he was a champion of absolute freedom of thought throughout his whole life.

Mounet Sully had taken him as a young man under his wing and they went about a lot together. In my view they must have been at one on the subject of purity. For one day Mounet who, it seems, was extremely candid, asked the young Granval who in his opinion was the best actor in the world.

Granval looked at him intently and said: "Master, it is Nijinski."

He had a biting wit and it was no good trying to parry it. He touched you with every stroke. You just had to acknowledge the touch.

He acted comedy marvellously, but he quickly tired of it . . . unless it was that he liked it too much and the slightest unpleasant detail close to him robbed him of his joy.

He painted as effectively as he acted. When he put on a play he could do the décor and costumes himself and needed no one's advice about the music.

He was erudite without being an intellectual. He gave the impression of not doing any of the things that he was doing; but when one knew him well one could see that that impression was the result of infinite pains and unobtrusive perseverance.

Above all he understood the actor admirably. At the time of my third show—*Hunger* and Laforgue's *Hamlet*—it was Granval who produced *Hamlet*. The stage adaptation of Laforgue's *Hamlet* was his in any case. He hadn't added a single word, but had simply done an enormous, skilful and reverent job with scissors.

The work I did under his direction in Laforgue's *Hamlet* was extremely precious to me. To all that I had attempted up till then

PIERRE CABANNE: Jean-Louis Barrault in *Les Fausses Confidences*

he brought *art*. Art, that is to say, choice; manner, taste, lack of taste when necessary; choice, in fact.

Say someone gives you a briar. You, with overall, a pair of secateurs, a cutting from some mysterious rose-bush, a knife, a length of raffia, a cigarette dangling carelessly from your mouth, and the air of thinking about something completely different, can make from this briar a rose-tree which will bear the blooms of Hadeleys, Edith Helens, Kordès and Madame Herriots.

That was the sort of gardener Granval was.

He loosened me up and put me on the road to diction. He showed me what true technique was. Later when I belonged to the Comédie Française I realised to what extent Granval was the exact representative of that illustrious house, that house born of the marriage between the traditional spirit deriving from the Hôtel de Bourgogne and the modern spirit brought by Molière's company. Granval was the prototype of the great tradition in harmony with the avant-garde spirit. From these two apparently hostile tendencies Granval achieved a synthesis.

My ambition from then onwards was also directed towards that synthesis and in that respect Granval, in spite of himself, influenced me considerably. He was a master.

But Granval never made much noise. By reason of his physical health he was a '*maître Hamlétique*', in Laforgue's words. He was a chaste man.

He made me understand the meaning of the word quality.

Granval was an artist in the state of grace.

9

Hunger

THE 1938–1939 season.
In the summer of 1938 I did a period of military training at Mailly. It was the Munich period. I already had in mind the idea of adapting Knut Hamsun's book, *Hunger*.

I had first come across Knut Hamsun's work in 1933, during my year of military service. Madeleine Milhaud had sent to the young soldier that I was Giono's *Jean le Bleu*—one of his best—and Knut Hamsun's *Mysteries* which utterly absorbed me.

And since then I had devoured *Vagabonds*, *Pan*, *Victoria*, and so on, and most of all, *Hunger*.

Hunger is concerned with a theme that should certainly have rung a deep bell within me, for it is the same as that of Kafka's *Trial*: the solitude of man within society. And another problem that always stirs me to the depths: *the problem of the double*. William Blake, Edgar Allan Poe, Baudelaire, etc. "The Marriage of Heaven and Hell."

Moreover *Hunger's* theme gave me the chance to put over on to the stage a fever that had consumed me for years and that I sometimes tried to calm with quinine. Quinine had given me acute noises in my ears; while the fever revealed to me the sharp beating of my heart. 'Hunger', which was not unknown to me, had caused me to undergo those periods of hallucination that struck me as being so dramatic and owing to which the subject sometimes borders on the waking dream. Finally Knut Hamsun's theme gave me the opportunity of attacking my art from its most extreme, if not impossible, side. One man and his double at grips with a cruelly organised collectivity. With that theme I could throw a challenge at the very substance of drama; it was a theme that touched the limit of the theatre's possibilities, a border-line case. But in mathematics don't we often discover solutions along these lines?

And again, the climate of the north appealed to me. If *As I Lay Dying* was my act of faith, and *Numantia* my first production, *Hunger* was my first attempt at a personal affirmation, my first shot at total theatre.

Masson was with me again for the costumes. As in *Numantia* I revelled in the elaboration of the dramatic arrangement of the décor. Marcel Delannoy, who had many ideas in common with us concerning total theatre, composed the music.

Once the play was written I had to get it passed by Knut Hamsun's translator. I read this gentleman the play I had extracted from the novel. He was satisfied with my adaptation and gave me leave to put on *Hunger*.

Hard facts: the budget for *Hunger* and Laforgue's *Hamlet* was 70,000 francs, but this time I didn't lose it all, for whereas *As I Lay Dying* was performed only six times, and *Numantia* fifteen, *Hunger* was played over fifty times.

The main reproach levelled against me by some of the key critics was that of being too like the post-war German theatre. They spoke of Piscatore. I had never seen any German plays nor anything by Piscatore, but from what I had been told I was if anything rather flattered.

In the meantime I had been seeing Dullin again, having acted in his production of Salacrou's *La Terre est Ronde*.

At that time he looked on me as a possible successor. Dullin wanted to leave the Atelier, and we had a long and serious conversation.

He told me he wanted to take over the Sarah-Bernhardt Theatre, and that in that case he would be leaving the Atelier, but he loved the Atelier so much that he didn't want to cut himself off from it altogether and not know what was going on there. He asked me if I was interested in the idea of taking his place at the Atelier. I answered that it would be my very greatest reward, and that I would do everything in my power to be worthy of my master. "May I ask what sort of line you would follow at the Atelier?" I reflected and then said: "The pre-*Volpone* one." He looked at me out of the corner of his eye and said: "You are perfectly right. I should have left at the *Volpone* period." Was he wrong or right? That is not the point. What I had let myself say about *Volpone* was based on various considerations.

Up to the time of *Volpone* the Atelier had shown several plays a year. A regular clientele had thus been formed (the sort of clientele I myself had seen the beginnings of with *Numantia* and *Hunger*). This clientele came automatically to see the Atelier's work and never missed a single production. It was this clientele, in fact, that assured the theatre its life.

Then came *Volpone's* success. The Atelier played *Volpone* 500 times running. What happened? The faithful clientele lost the habit of going regularly to the Atelier. It was replaced temporarily by a passing clientele, the one that always chases after successes. And when *Volpone's* first and too-long run came to an end, the success-seeking clientele, the passing one, did not come back to see the next play for its interest lay in the *play* and not the deep activity of the Atelier, yet at the same time the former regular clientele, the basic one, had lost the habit of making its way up the little Rue Dancourt.

Volpone, by its very success, had cut the Atelier off from a section of its habitués.

This situation made me think for the first time of the solution of Alternation. If Dullin at that time had been able to practise alternation, *Volpone* would have remained on the placards and its success been exploited, while the deep activity of the Atelier would have not been thereby threatened, as happened with *Volpone's* 500-day run.

So when war overtook us I had plans with Dullin which both alarmed and delighted me. But life said No to that solution.

Hunger was liked. Dullin liked it, Decroux liked it whereas he had felt very bitter about *As I Lay Dying* and had roundly criticised *Numantia*. So there must have been some progress. But my greatest encouragement came from Paul Claudel who wrote me his first letter.

Looking back on it I like the First Act best (the nightmare night in the bedroom) and the end of the play, particularly the scene in which the person was shipped off. For that there was a dialogue between the written word and a chant intoned through closed lips which conveyed mystery and prolongation.

To the dramatic action as a whole I had applied a method of plastic interplay which considerably increased the possibilities of changing the location, of the rapid establishing of an atmosphere, of striking foreshortenings. But to me this plastic material was a means, a freer and broader means towards dramatic movement.

So when these innovations—such as a given way of going up steps—gained immediate success and won applause as a 'stunt' would, I was not pleased. This novel way of moving on the stage was for me merely a new form of style which freed the general dramatic expression without falsifying the basic end—which was to understand the *natures* and, broadly speaking, the *adventures of men*. But the success of this new style gave a visual emphasis to the production at the expense of its native dramatic qualities.

The play struck some people as strange, and, being strange, as foreign to the normal and recognised activity of the theatre. But to me it was perfectly normal theatre. The fact was that the public was not yet accustomed to it (any more than the actors were, for that matter). The novelty made its effect but confined the style of the production within a 'special' atmosphere, and that irritated me quite a bit.

Since then the public has made great progress. I observed it in the small attention given to certain bold effects in *Le Soulier de Satin*.

By then, and although it was in the Théâtre Français, people were getting used to that manner. It was because the manner did not arouse attention that progress was made.

My first attempt at total theatre—by which I mean life

Baptiste pantomime de J-Louis Barrault

Mayo: sketch for *Baptiste*

83

transmitted to the stage by means of the *total* utilisation of all the means of expression at the disposal of a Human Being and the *total* utilisation of his whole range of musical and plastic expression (song, lyrical diction, prose diction, cries, breathing, sighs, silences, prosaic bodily expression, the art of gesture, symbolic gesture, lyrical gesture and dance)—presented a problem, that of training actors specifically with that technique in view.

For in fact there is no school that inculcates that technique and no actor in our country who is really trained for it. Hence total theatre quite simply posits the problem of the teaching and re-education of all the actors of the West.

It has often been remarked that our stage is cluttered up by too much décor and too much music, that our theatre is too much 'a meeting-place of the arts'.

It has often been said that the theatre is first and foremost a finely-written play to be well spoken by good actors and that everything else is generally superfluous.

It occurs to me that it has never been realised that defence against excessive music and décor will be achieved only when what is conveyed by the excessive music and décor can be replaced by means of authentic theatre.

That a serviceable but foreign art, as are painting and music, should have to come to the rescue of our productions is ample proof that these, if stripped of all accessories and taken alone, do not make the required impact on the audience.

If the actor were really a double character, if he could be himself and his part at one and the same time, the décor would automatically be reduced to its proper rôle: its function would become essentially dramatic. A bit of wall for an interior, a banister to indicate stairs, a valuable stage property representing a horse's head, a branch to signify a forest, and a single chair for the actor to sit down upon.

The décor of a ballet is dictated by the dance; the dance imposes the style of the décor. The dance has the décor it deserves. And it is the same with the theatre. Our present-day theatre has the décor it deserves, and if it is invariably overladen it is because the actors themselves don't furnish enough of the properties.

If we want one day to reduce the décor to its proper limits, a technique must be acquired by which the acting of the actors will replace what is normally provided by the décor.

The problem of the décor, then, depends on the technical ability of the company.

All attempts to act in front of a curtain with the elements of décor reduced to their simplest have broken down. They were pleasing for a time, while they were new, but since the reduction of décor was replaced by nothing at all, a 'lack' was soon felt, and built décor logically returned to take its place and clutter up, yes, most definitely, the stage.

Here is an interesting quotation from Chateaubriand on the subject.

> Precision in representing inanimate objects is the spirit of the literature and arts of our time, and it proclaims the decadence of great poetry and true drama. We are content with small beauties when we are incapable of large ones; we copy, to deceive the eye, armchairs and velvet when we are no longer able to paint the aspect of the man seated on the velvet and in the armchairs.
>
> However, once we have descended to this realistic depiction of material form, we are compelled to go on reproducing it, for the public, having become materialist, demands it.

Our theories, having arrived at their logical conclusion of total theatre, as I was saying, found themselves up against the problem of a new technique for the actor. For there exists in the West no school capable of forming actors of this kind.

Many people will say, so much the better. To which we can only reply: then let's abandon our attempt at total theatre and go back, not to tradition—for until the Renaissance and during part of the seventeenth and eighteenth centuries, and ever since antiquity, there existed nothing but total theatre, real total theatre—but to the theatre of the last century, to that tradition, the so-called 'bourgeois' theatre, the 'hands in the pockets' theatre, as Lucien Guitry called it.

But if we do want to face up to the problem of the true tradition—call it total theatre or what you will—then we will have first and foremost to face up to the problem of the actor.

That must have been more or less my state of mind as regards the theatre at that period.

In July, after a cure at Vichy, I went to visit Paul Claudel. My first visit to him at Brangues. And I asked him for *Tête d'Or, Partage de Midi* and *Le Soulier de Satin.*

He readily gave me *Tête d'Or* which he hadn't re-read, he said, for forty years and which in his opinion must be unreadable.

He refused me *Partage de Midi* saying he would let me have it only after his death.

He said that the *Soulier* must be done in its entirety.

And he talked to us—to Madeleine and myself—about *L'Annonce*. By this interview our 'connaissance' was furthered: 'co-naissance' or better 're-connaissance', as he said.

On 25 August I, and others like me, were called up. As a 'specialist' (specialist of what, my God!).

Monstrous absurdity had got the better of human intelligence. I observed that men accept war above all because most of them are so bored with life. For myself, it was into boredom that I was plunged.

"More dark and dark our woes!" (Romeo).

1

Miramont de Quercy

MIRAMONT is the little village in Quercy where we landed up in July, 1940. Purposeless, prostrated.

I had been posted during the war to a company where there were quite a few painters. At the time when I had thought of becoming a painter I had studied at the École du Louvre.

On my military papers I was: artist. At the moment, whether painter, gun-carriage-driver or engineer, I was, like all the others, quite shattered.

While awaiting demobilisation we went for long walks in a countryside that was both wild and restrained. One day when I and my friend, the painter Planson, were going for one of these walks and trying to recast our ideas I said: "It will be quite impossible for me to pick up my old independent life for some years to come. From the social point of view it will be impossible for me to express my opinions and the sort of thing I would want to do will inevitably be forbidden. That is how things stand from the moral point of view. Technically, however, things are different. By now I have probably lost the little I had learned, and what I would like to do is to start from the beginning again, get down to study again in honest and really first-class surroundings. I know! I'd like to join the Comédie Française, and spend five or six years there learning my true craft at last. The Comédie Française could be that irreproachably honest and first-class school."

Of course I said all that among thousands of other things, as happens when one lets one's mind wander in complete freedom strolling along with a friend. But no one knew where we were. Madeleine Renaud was in Brittany. We were separated by the line of demarcation.

In my general muddle I also imagined myself founding a theatrical company in Aix-en-Provence. It was Aix that I chose without particularly knowing anything about Aix.

I heard that J. Copeau was acting as stopgap for Edouard Bourdet in the administration of the Comédie Française, but I didn't see that this had any bearing on anything else. And supposing I had seen, I would have thought: "Why should the Comédie Française take me on at this point, when I am run down, out of training, and have forgotten everything I ever knew?" And a hundred kindred thoughts.

On 28 July I was given my liberty and I landed up at Toulouse with my 800 francs demobilisation money. No one could go up to Paris yet, through Vierzon, at which point one made one's first contact with the forces of Occupation.

I mooned about. A few days passed, two or three. Pierre Dac, whom I met, kindly came to my help. I also came across Charles Wolff, who was quite wild. It was the last time I saw him.

And then suddenly I met Monsieur Fleury, the cashier of the Français.

"What on earth are you doing here?" he said. "You're being looked for everywhere."

"Me?"

"Yes. I've had a message from Copeau. He wants you. He wants to engage you for the Français."

"Me?"

"Yes. Can't you hear?"

"Er—yes!"

Copeau was looking for me to engage me at the Français?

"He wants a Rodrigue so as to put on the *Cid*."

Me? Rodrigue? (Never perhaps had I felt less heroic. The Spanish Rodrigue, yes, under pressure, but this bull of Corneille's . . .)

Whoever you are, if you are ever given the opportunity of entering the Comédie Française, take it! That is the advice I have always given since.

CHRISTIAN BÉRARD: costumes for the *chevaux de la nuit* in *Amphitryon*

90

Fleury let Copeau know that I was found. On 9 August I crossed over the line.

On 16 August I signed up, and when I finally found Madeleine Renaud we both belonged, at last, to the same theatre!

I relate this brief story in homage to my Star. That is what I call being protected in life. Though it can be confoundedly binding, for really one is hardly a free agent when protected to quite such an extent! All my life I have been aware of an invisible presence tenderly putting me on my path. A secret brother leading me along. And what's more all my life I have obeyed him. May he not bear me a grudge if one day I fail to do so.

Life with or without this secret presence is tantamount to going shooting with or without a dog.

The dog, the trusty pointer, who leads you where your bird has fallen and warns you instantly of its presence. But if we want to keep a pointer such as this we have to see to it that we are worthy of it.

I have a friend to whom an excellently trained dog was lent at a shooting party. The dog flushed the partridges, my friend fired and missed. The dog turned and looked at him in surprise. A few minutes later the dog started a hare, my friend shot and missed. The dog turned round and gave him a black look. A third time the dog started some other game, my friend shot and missed. That time the dog did neither the first nor the second, but went back to his kennel despite the clumsy sportsman's threats.

The problem lies in not letting our pointer down. Therein lies the difficulty. I could tell eight, ten, twelve anecdotes illustrating my Guide's exploits. Sometimes he takes me by the hand and drags me; sometimes he holds me back. Sometimes he puts *signs* on my path for my attention.

"All is not illusion, but allusion," said Claudel.

Long may I have the illusion of those allusions.

In joining the Comédie Française I began my life anew. It was not a new life but the same one differently treated, that's all, like a second version of the same play.

G

2

La Comédie Française

I WAS proud and happy to belong to the Comédie Française in however small a capacity. I set out anew and my life started again as if I was a second generation of myself.

I experienced a recrudescence of my old terrors; my 'stage fright' returned. The timidity of my earliest days again took hold of me, and also my fanatical faculty for self-recollection.

The Comédie Française teems with awe-inspiring *Shades*. Say that you have Fabian's four lines to read in *Polyeucte* which merely provide those tried princes of the stage—who were at that time the *sociétaires* of the Français—with their cues, then you are given a splendid and weighty breastplate lined with a sort of saltpetre deposited there by the sweat of ages, and on the label beside the index number—like in the Bibliothèque Nationale—you see the name 'De Max'. And you are at your ease forthwith!

Say you are given the part of the guard in the *Misanthrope*, then a costume embroidered with pearls and as heavy as lead is doled out to you, giving you an air of the period—complete with all the undergarments, so that when you are finally rigged out you feel you really have stepped into the reign of Louis XIV.

Then there is the bench in the concierge's office which still bears the traces of De Max's Shade. And in the Café de la Régence there survives the thundering Shade of Paul Mounet. And near the stage there is the bust of Worms. And the corridors still re-echo with Silvain's exquisite repartees.

The craftsman side of me which makes me love the professional protocol, and the side of me that needs to show respect for those who know, were happy at the Français. What a queer anarchist I am, aren't I?

The intense joy of going, as soon as I had joined, to pay my respects to the *doyen*. At the Français the *doyen* is the oldest *sociétaire*, not the oldest actor. One must get that right.

The curious thing was that my first untamed formative years fitted very well into this ancestral hierarchy. I have always been exhilarated by the peculiar atmosphere arising from great old houses where craftsmen are at work. And although I am perfectly capable of playing truant when injustice gets the upper hand, I feel very near to the guild spirit of the Middle Ages when life suddenly comes straight again. The reconciling of Saint-Just with St. Louis.

The first thing that enraptured me at the Comédie Française was the smell of the boards. The time-worn mellowness of the vaulting, the extraordinary impression conveyed by a place 'where work is done'. Contrary to what is usually supposed, dust would be unthinkable there. The very amount of work done prevents dust getting a hold. If dust lies anywhere it is on the minds of some of the *sociétaires* who naïvely imagine that they are serving their House. The Comédie Française, sheerly as an instrument, is the least dusty object I have ever seen. In virtue of the amount of work exacted the professional spirit alone reigns. The Comédie Française is the very spirit of our profession.

The quantity and variety of the work it has to achieve day by day makes the technical staff the best-trained that exists. Moreover among all the souls that serve the Français, that is the section most sensitive to the *Shades*. Hence it is the best trained.

In my very early days I was present when a dresser, Augustine, had to retire at the age of eighty-two after sixty-two years of service in the Théâtre Français. She had dressed Reichenberg.

In the normal way the Past saddens me and the Future fills me with fear. Only the knowledge of really belonging to a profession, of being able, indeed compelled, to contribute my share to it— only that can procure me a holy joy. As if it were a matter of religion. Past, Present, Future then form a continuity like a chain unwinding itself in time and of which I am a link, a mere link. The perennialness of my profession softens my personal anguish.

It is only with the passage of time that a conscientiously-run enterprise can leave a really flawless deposit. And this deposit constitutes a sort of hall-mark of integrity before which even sincere cheating becomes impossible. The Comédie Française in the course of its 250 years has become a filter that lets nothing through. Its judgment is implacable.

If its God is still Molière, the real head of the Church was Lagrange.

It has had its warlike Popes like Le Kain, its turbulent ones like Talma, its eccentric saints like Rachel, its high-priests like Mounet, and also its faithful servants—solid country parish priests—like Got.

'L'illustre Théâtre' is its catacomb period. . . .

But until the first world war it contrived, or anyway was able, to keep spiritually apart from the State. We shall revert to this point.

I had never before had occasion to rehearse on such a large stage nor within so vast a structure. J. Copeau really had engaged me to play Rodrigue. Personally I would never have chosen Rodrigue for my début. But it was a matter of contract and I had blind faith in Copeau.

Copeau's method—an excellent one that I myself have followed, the method of Stanislawski and of the *Cartel*—was to begin rehearsals by assembling the cast round a table for the first week or so. Each one speaks his part and agreement is reached as to the reading of the text. But even there, round the table, I hardly dared raise my voice, lost among the famous names of the stage.

The day of the first rehearsal on the stage came only too soon and I found myself alone in the immense building with the Cid's famous lines before me. . . .

After the third line I was drained dry. My lungs were emptied as if they had been sucked in by the huge and monstrously dark theatre.

What had become of my First breathing and my Second

PIERRE CABANNE: Jean-Louis Barrault and Maria Casarès in *L'État de Siège*

95

breathing? Surrounded by this true professionalism, what had happened to all my fine theories?

I stopped and shamefacedly asked if my lines could be skipped. I had to go and think in a corner.

The whole thing was quite simply stage fright, and before long I had proved that my two sorts of breathing, the one that serves the actor and the one that serves his part, did really exist. In the trade it is called being able to '*soutenir*' or, more graphically, having '*dessous*'. My First breathing was nothing other than the breathing of 'support', the 'underlying reserve'.

I experienced, too, the equivalent of Volpone's bed.

One evening after we had played I can't now remember what, I dived down into the metro like everyone else.

I had my ticket punched and was waiting for my train.

When suddenly a flood of love swept up into my breast; to hell with my ticket! I ran up the stairs again, four at a time, and plunged into the Théâtre Français, which was not yet shut, and slipped into the auditorium. I was in the Darkness and Silence of that well of exacting demands.

The identical self-recollection of my night at the Atelier. . . . The same potential faces, the same creakings, the same interior murmurings, the same secret whisperings all around me.

Only the size of the setting was different. It was bigger, which was natural after ten years.

"How small this wash-house is. . . ."

Primitive desire for Prayer. Love of the craft.

A burglar, an aesthetic burglar, once told me that he felt a fetishistic adoration for his jemmy similar to that of the savage for his arrows (or some other noble object of the kind).

One evening I dined with a big industrialist who built ships and who spent the whole meal pitying me because of my profession. A profession which, he said, consisted in smearing one's face like a girl, putting on fancy-dress as it if was carnival, and repeating the same words every evening . . . "and not your own words at that." I said: "You, sir, build ships. Very well. If you lost several million francs per ship built, granting that it wouldn't break you financially, would you go on building ships?" "No, if I lost millions in building ships I would stop." "Very well, sir, then you don't really love building ships. As for me, if I lost my life acting I would still go on acting. Which proves that I love my craft more than you love yours." I should add that this little exchange bound us together and we went along full sail for the rest of the evening.

Greatness is arrived at by the gate of the familiar. As soon as we have rooted out the familiar recesses of a thing we are well on the way to evaluating its greatness. That night I familiarised myself with the inside of the Français.

Yes, all the great things are familiar. Valéry is familiar. Claudel is familiar. Shakespeare, Mòlière: all the great men are familiar. They reach the height of what they are touching.

The familiar angle of a great thing, there lies the riddle.

In the darkness and silence of the theatre I sought the familiar angle. At any rate an intimate relationship was established between the theatre and myself, a secret understanding, something like an act of love, so much so that the next day when I was there with the others, there was a sort of complicity between the theatre and myself. Henceforth we had our secret, and who knows whether my eyes looked different?

"You could see it in his face!"

I got to know about the *rhythm of alternation* and could see for myself how profitable it is for an actor to move from one part to another. It knocks the corners off him, supples him up, prevents him from forming habits. He learns to work quickly and if he knows how to remain true and steer clear of a false craft (there lies the one but grave pitfall), he becomes the 'affective-athlete' about which Antonin Artaud speaks in *Le Théâtre et son Double*.

I realised that the alternating rhythm is the most vital formula of our trade.

But being 'new' I acted little, and acting too little I strained at the leash.

And then I went on tour quite a bit in the great and small towns of the occupied zone. I played what the occasion offered.

Some of my parts made me have to *fight my pride*. Gringoire, among others, was good for me. He forced me to lay my own personal tastes aside and made the actor in me plead for a play that the artist in me disapproved of, at least in part. That was excellent practice. An actor should be able to play a part in a work he dislikes. An actor is an advocate, the counsel for the defence. Now it sometimes happens that the counsel for the defence has to plead the innocence of someone whom he knows to be guilty. If the counsel is a good actor, he succeeds in convincing. And if the actor is a good advocate, he wins.

To give an example of what I mean: In my opinion Banville as a poet is superior to his Gringoire.

I like his definition of poetry: "It consists in arranging words among themselves, words that fill the ear like persistent music, or as best they can paint everything from life, and among them there are sometimes twin sounds that pair off and seem to chime together madly, like golden bells."

Modern poetry!

He was something of a forerunner, and I understand that Rimbaud sent his first poems to Banville.

I also came into contact with the *teaching at the Conservatoire* and was able to compare it with the teaching at the independent schools.

There is something mysterious about the Conservatoire teaching. If the independent schools seem to draw especial attention to the broad art of the theatre, the Conservatoire's emphasis seems in fact to lie on the formation of the actor.

The Conservatoire pupil learns to pitch his voice more quickly. (Sometimes so quickly that it gets pitched too far forward and is falsified; he gets given a voice out of tune with the instrument with which his nature corresponds.)

The Conservatoire pupil is a young actor who can be heard and understood. He does not always act his situation fully, contenting himself with merely giving his answers. Sometimes when he has finished speaking he stops acting. He waits his turn; but when it falls to him to speak again his voice is placed, he can be heard and understood.

Why is it so different with the independent schools? Does the fault lie with the teachers or the method of teaching Yet I have known excellent teachers in the independent schools, and the teaching method of the Conservatoire isn't so marvellous as all that. So what?

Oh, those learned schools that can benefit from the ever-growing experience of generation after generation! It was through coming into contact with the Conservatoire and its teaching that I again became fascinated by the teaching problem. Most definitely the technique of the actor gets me!

I discovered the mute 'e'.

In 1761 Voltaire wrote as follows to Monsieur Deodati of Tovazzi who had vaunted the excellence of the Italian tongue at the expense of the French:

"You reproach us with our mute e's calling them a sad and hollow sound that dies away on our lips. But it is precisely in our mute e's that the great harmony of our prose and poetry lies: *empire, couronne, diadème, flamme, tendresse, victoire*. All these happy word-endings leave a sound that lingers on in the ear after the word has been uttered, like a clavichord which goes on resounding after the fingers have left the keys."

And sometimes I got a glimpse into the *lyrical state*; the 'expansion of the soul' which makes the whole Being become rhythm.

I had penetrated the Palace of the great craft. My eyes never tired of contemplating its riches.

At the Comédie Française there is a big difference between the *pensionnaire* and the *sociétaire*, and the whole difference is that whereas the *pensionnaire* is taken on *by the year*, the *sociétaire* is under contract for LIFE.

The position of the *pensionnaire* is the same as that of all actors under contract by the year in a regular company. One or other party can cancel the contract at the end of a year, due notice having been given.

The position of the *sociétaire* is, on the other hand, very special. The *sociétaire* can never be dismissed. He can only retire, and that only after twenty years. He can never go back. He has a share in the business. His whole life long he can never recover his liberty. He is on the one hand bound *for life* to the destiny of the Société des Comédiens Français of which he is, on the other hand, one of the co-directors.

My state of mind at the Français, I must confess, was always rather disturbed. My joys there were complete, but they were rare. I was tossed between ecstasy and frustration.

I had shortly before made the acquaintance of Jean-Paul Sartre who had just written *Les Mouches*. In one of my moments of unfulfilled desires I had for the first time visited the Marigny Theatre. At another time the Athénée. Jean-Paul Sartre and I wanted to put on *Les Mouches*, but first of all *Le Soulier de Satin*. Jean-Paul Sartre had a special predilection for *Le Soulier de Satin*. "I would leave the Français and take over a theatre myself . . ." But then the Français got hold of me again by one of those periods of utter bliss and I gave up my projects. And so it was that I couldn't put on *Les Mouches*. I hope one day to make up for it.

I wavered. I was happy and dissatisfied at the same time. At the committee meetings at the end of 1942 A. Brunot, the *doyen*, representing the Société, approached me about becoming a *sociétaire*. My agony grew. My hesitation wasn't half-and-half. No! it was all-or-nothing.

The joy of giving oneself Wholly to the magnificent cause of the Société des Comédiens Français. I say "Wholly" deliberately.

LUCIEN COUTAUD: décor for *Le Soulier de Satin*

Wholly and not by halves. The desire, indeed the need, to give my Whole self to the profession I had chosen.

It was obvious to me that I could not serve my profession better than in the very heart of the Société des Comédiens Français, but in the heart of the Société, could I give myself utterly?

And I was as hungry as a wolf.

Accepting the offer of a *sociétariat* meant committing oneself *for life*; it was no laughing matter. And I had to decide. I sent a letter to the Administrator, J.-L. Vaudoyer, in which I refused. Clearly I refused with death in my heart. Refusal meant that I must leave. . . .

And while J.-L. Vaudoyer was making my decision known to the committee I had gone to have a drink opposite, at the Univers, with a fanatically avant-garde friend.

That was the world that I would automatically go back to. Try-outs, innovations, experiments, and without the controlling force that the Français represented. Illusory truths, irregularities. . . .

A more exciting life, certainly, and in a sense a more poetic one. "We must live dangerously!" Yes, but that applies to poets and writers, to people who are artists only, not to people who are artist and instrument at the same time. Liberty and fantasy are for the artist. The instrument must have the discipline of an athlete. So the choice was: art for art's sake, exclusively: or the life of the artist for its own personal pleasures? The monk or the anarchist?

The conversation at the Univers was decisive, for suddenly seized with panic I left my friend, dashed into the Français and gave Emile, the head commissionaire, a message to take up to the committee room to the effect that if it was not now too late I would accept a *sociétariat*.

Man is sensitive, and the actor is particularly sensitive to that sensitivity; someone opened the door, I went in, I burst into tears, and everyone cried. In that warm salt water I saw the consummation of our fraternal association; for henceforth I would be an associate with them, a co-director with them of the Société des Comédiens Français. Just as my hesitation had been total, so was my 'taking of the veil' total, in intention. I firmly believe that my emotion turned into a vague defensive anger against anyone who might in the future rise up and imperil the general interest of the Société des Comédiens Français. If it had cost me so much to become a *sociétaire* it was because I had decided to be one through and through. I warned them: "I will show you . . . there will be no restraining me!" and so on. From tears we passed to laughter and from laughter to serious matters. Then I let them finish their work and sought refuge in the office of the stage director, dear Mathis, over with the technicians.

I had just committed myself FOR LIFE; the fat was in the fire. . . .

I had chosen the life of a Monk.

But not that of a sheeplike-monk

nor that of a civil-service-monk

but a sort of monk-militant.

FOR LIFE

But life said No to that.

Life is an odd person. And yet it is her odd side that makes me like her. The ideas she has for you up her sleeve!

It's that Destiny she's got herself tied up with!

3

Phèdre

*The mind of the ancients . . . is of a beauty
so male that to unmask its beauty you must
have a shrewd suspicion that it exists: simple
in its manner, I will not say that it has seen
the world, but* only have the courage to
want to love it *and in the end you will find
it charming.*

Said by Hortensius in Marivaux's
LA SECONDE SURPRISE DE L'AMOUR.

I DID not want to take on *Phèdre*. The fact was that I hardly dared to. I felt I was insufficiently acclimatised to the classical world to take over the production of the play and—more so —to direct others already versed in this form.

Ever since 1939 Marie Bell had been cast to play Phèdre. Edouard Bourdet and Jean Hugo had spread themselves over the décor and the costumes. The décor was already built and the sketches for the costumes existed.

So the framework was all there; there remained the task of filling it out. Marie Bell asked that I should do it; she had confidence in me, and I let myself be drawn in.

My thanks to Marie Bell for having influenced me to accept.

Phèdre, Racine, were to be a complete revelation to me. A classic is like hidden treasure. Its core is buried under so many layers of varnish, so many polishings, that it can be reached only by patience and infiltration. But once it is reached—or once we think it is—there are dazzling riches to be discovered at every turn. Its resources are inexhaustible.

But if we are to reach the inmost recesses of a classic, we must cultivate the methods and tenacity of a spelaeologist. And this, when all is said and done, is the only attitude of mind that can mature without losing its youth. But what abnegation it requires! It is a struggle 'to the death' between passion and taste, and how much we have to add to our stature to remain master of the situation!

Racine is perhaps the greatest and certainly the most musical of all our French poets. How elegantly he hides his power behind an alexandrine!

For me *Phèdre* opened the door on to the whole of Racine.

He is the most alive thing in the world, for since his death he has enjoyed the sacred privilege of living for us at each and every stage of his career. You and I call ourselves mortals probably because we die every day; what we were yesterday is dead, what we shall be to-morrow is still unborn. But Racine has lived again for us throughout these 250 years—wholly and simultaneously: the child playing in the gardens of Port Royal, the novice pirouetting to Uzès, the young man in revolt against his masters, the dramatic author living his season in hell, the mature man who has become the King's docile historiographer, the strict father writing severe letters to his son, and finally the aged poet singing the praises of the Lord among the girls at Saint-Cyr.

It is a multiple Racine that Racine offers us, for he is composed of as many characters as he put into his tragedies—characters that did not always agree with each other; so he offers us too as many conflicts as he had to wage with himself, within himself.

The spirit at war with the flesh, the flesh at war with the spirit—that is the eternal conflict. Baudelaire said later: "In every man, at every moment, there are two simultaneous postulations, one towards God and the other towards Satan. The desire to mount the scale confronted by the delights of descent."

Racine's dramatic work seems to lie in a parenthesis. A parenthesis opened by the Port Royal child of the Odes contemplating the "swallows skimming" over the surface of the lake, and closed by the same child, very pure, the one in *Athalie*: Joas, otherwise Eliacin. On either side lies the soul of a very pure child who, during the profane period of dramatic production, becomes: Astyanax, Britannicus, Iphigénie, and the two young people in *Phèdre*.[1]

Mon Dieu, quelle guerre cruelle!
Je trouve deux hommes en moi:
L'un veut que plein d'amour pour toi
Mon cœur te soit toujours fidèle.
L'autre à tes volontés rebelle
Me révolte contre ta loi.

L'un tout esprit, et tout céleste,
Veut qu'au ciel sans cesse attaché,
Et des biens éternels touché,
Je compte pour rien tout le reste;
Et l'autre par son poids funeste
Me tient vers la terre penché.

Hélas! en guerre avec moi-même,
Où pourrai-je trouver la paix?
Je veux, et n'accomplis jamais.
Je veux, mais ô misère extrême!
Je ne fais pas le bien que j'aime,
Et je fais le mal que je hais.

O grâce, ô rayon salutaire,
Viens me mettre avec moi d'accord;
Et domptant par un doux effort
Cet homme qui t'est si contraire,
Fais ton esclave volontaire
De cet esclave de la mort.

Depths from which a synthesised Racine will arise, holding aloft the Virgin and Child and, on the stage, reconciling the sacred and the profane.

[1] I would like one day to write a sort of study called: "Racine or Eliacin's Season in Hell."

BALTHUS: setting for *L'État de Siège*
107

Since embarking on *Phèdre* I have never been able to detach myself from Racine. I tried to note down all the problems *Phèdre* suggested to me in a study called *Commentaires sur Phèdre*.[1] There follow some extracts from it.

> *We cannot be too careful to put*
> *nothing on the stage but what is very*
> *necessary.*
> RACINE: Preface to *Mithridate*.

Concerning the Recitative

The recitative marks the entry of action into the specifically poetic world, the world of the waking-dream. It is the moment when man starts to 'think out loud'; the moment when exaltation is so tense and so extreme that it can express itself in song. The recitative is the actor's main stumbling-block, for he cannot recognise its necessity, cannot so to speak discover it, unless he himself has reached that higher state which is none other than the lyrical state. It is a phenomenon of extra-lucidity experienced in those moments when the creature is near ecstasy. The recitative brings a sudden change in the rhythm, a sort of change of gear which strangely slows down the delivery—comparable in mechanics to the changing of gear which suddenly causes a higher 'rev.' Suddenly the engine turns more slowly before gathering momentum. But this change of rhythm cannot take place without the intermediary of a normal switch-over. Just as the clutch is indispensable to the changing of gear, the recitative, if it is to impose itself and be "very necessary", in Racine's words, cannot appear but by the natural phenomenon of a sort of mental disengagement comparable to delirium.

There is a modern machine that gives a fairly good illustration of the recitative—I mean the aeroplane at the moment of taking off. The machine taxies over the ground. The engine goes flat out, all its strength mustered to reach its maximum power. It

---

[1] Éditions du Seuil.

bumps frantically over the rough ground giving all the symptoms of tortured agitation; an absolute climax of vitality and movement.

Then suddenly and surprisingly we see a strange calm come over it; we imagine it to be still on the ground, but it seems to have stopped moving, stopped making an effort. A moment of hesitation, renouncement, a sort of neutral plane in which all movement seems to have vanished.

But soon we see that the aeroplane is rising, leaving us behind. It has left the ground. Now it is gaining height, flying away. The recitative is beginning.

When it has made its flight it comes down again and at the moment of landing we can observe the brutal return of movement. The recitative is almost always bounded by two periods of violent agitation. So this is the pattern:

1. Feverish activity.
2. The queer plane of indecision, the brusque rupture in the rhythm, the briefest pause in which the character finds a new rhythm.
3. The flight proper of the recitative, its curve and fall.
4. Finally, the sudden reversion to activity.

A natural illustration of the recitative can also be found in certain extreme situations in daily life.

Whoever has had the misfortune to watch beside the body of some beloved person will trace in the following the embryonic idea of the recitative. Near the body sits the watcher, sobbing chokingly. His grief is almost hysterical; he is half strangled. When suddenly he stops, pulls himself together, and appears to have become calm. Weak with grief as he is, he rallies his strength sufficiently to sing the praises of the deceased. Why was he so distressed? His eulogies rise up, his heart soars, every ideal is attributed to the loved one; no virtue is passed over, no admirable action unsung. But in the graph that he is describing he finally comes to the loved one's illness and is once more faced with the death that snatched him away. He is down to earth again, face to face with reality. Immediately the hopeless sobbing starts up; for a second time he is at the mercy of the painful agitation that threatens to break him.

Concerning perfect chords

There are some alexandrines which in themselves constitute true and perfect chords. Sometimes they serve as support at the outset of the recitative but usually they are to be found at its climax.

Reflections on the Voice

The voice must be able to cope with a certain form of speech that is neither prose nor song. The actor must be able to 'pitch' his voice, like a singer, but he must also be able to 'unpitch' it. When the voice-specialist pitches his voice he makes use, preferably, of all the resonant cavities and pipes at the top of the head.

Such a voice-specialist (be he singer, barrister, preacher or actor) is commonly said to have his voice pitched 'in the head' (a 'head voice'). But there are other resonant pipes and cavities, such as the thoracic cage, the pharynx and the mouth, etc. Usually a voice-specialist selects certain cavities (the 'head' ones for example) and develops these to the maximum (as flowers are 'forced' in a hothouse) so that he can 'project' his voice further. Now the actor should be able to pass from one kind of resonance to the other. There should be no divorce between the timbre of his voice and the breath of his life. For the singer it is the note that matters; for the preacher the volume of the church and the distance between himself and his faithful. As for the barrister he is almost an actor. For the actor what matters is a true reconstruction of life. He should be able without fatigue to pass from one voice-position to another. He should be able to 'unpitch' his voice.

If the singer's voice is an instrument, the actor's is an orchestra. The actor, in the shifting of his voice-positions, should make different instruments vibrate—his strings, his woodwind, his brass and even his percussion. It is in this way that life is manifest, that the actor reveals his presence.

In everyday life men, like actors (or rather actors, like men) use the cavities of the mouth, the pharynx, the Eustachian tubes, the sinuses and the thoracic cage in the pitching of their voices. They do it subconsciously, depending on events. Thus the voice seems to go right down into the chest under the influence of amorous desire (it unpitches itself); whereas it comes up and vibrates in the nose under the influence of fear; when it is being authoritative it makes use of the roof of the mouth, and so on.

The actor should know about these continual shiftings of the voice and it would be useful if there were a solfeggio of voice-positions by which the actor could train himself and acquire greater voice-agility. Then it would come easily to him to let his breath strike the upper lip, the palate, the throat or the bottom lip, regions which correspond respectively to the nervous, intellectual, sensual and digestive centres.[1] A whole system of scales could be worked out by which the actor could acquire an outstandingly agile and 'present' voice.

Articulation

Actors should also be given 'studies' rather like musical 'studies'—if only that they might gain a deeper awareness of the *crescendo*, of the enormous effort required to describe a pretty *diminuendo*, of the *sforzando*, the *staccato*, the *legato*; of a tied note, a dotted note, a quaver, etc.

There are passages that should 'flow' like a *legato*; others that should be syl-la-bil-ised. And there are those progressive losings of breath that recall the *diminuendo* and 'fading-out' of the wireless.

---

[1] Hence my study of *Phèdre* led me back to the work I was envisaging with Artaud.

Concerning Gesture

> The gesticulation of the actors seemed
> to command their arms and their robes
> to be majestic. But the rebellious limbs
> flaunted a biceps between the shoulder
> and the elbow that knew nothing at all
> about the part it was intended to play.
>   MARCEL PROUST

The verbal form of tragedy is no ordinary form, it is the alexandrine. The alexandrine is based on Number. Thus the alexandrine is not spoken in an ordinary way, but its speech is governed by the rhythm of Number.

The way in which the action unfolds is not ordinary either. From among an epitomised selection the actions have been sifted and purified. They have a circular form and play upon each other in accordance with perfect symmetry. The action of a tragedy is a pure geometrical figure.

In writing his tragedies Racine obeyed the exacting demands of Number and pure geometry. The virtues essential to a classical work are Measure and Design.

The actor, too, does his best to obey Number in his diction. At all events he recognises it. Moreover his conduct has to be in accordance with that imposed by the author. Hence both in his actions and his speech he does not conduct himself in an ordinary way.

Up to this point, then, the purity of dramatic art is safe-guarded. The language is elliptic, the action is 'crystallised'. If this purity is to be absolutely safeguarded the actor must also move in a way that is not ordinary. His gesticulation, like the alexandrines he utters and the conduct he pursues, must be calculated, chosen, rhythmic. If this is not so, what happens?

Any transition from gesture to speech becomes impossible, for a synthesis of what is seen and what is heard cannot take place. The 'chemical precipitate' of this delicate artistic operation cannot come about. The theatrical phenomenon ceases to exist.

We no longer know where we are. If we think we are in ordinary life then we wonder why the characters speak and conduct themselves in such an extraordinary way. If, on the other hand, we persist in our idea that the stage is a magical place, a mysterious casket of illusions, then it disturbs us to see such ordinary characters moving about on it.

It is because of this sudden weakness that many people think the theatre an impure art, vulgar and second-rate.

The public, accustomed to plastic naturalism, is usually bored by tragedy; it falls asleep to the rhythm of the alexandrines. But what it should do is to hoot at the 'false notes' traced in the air by actors ignorant of gesticulation just as it would hoot with horror on hearing a discordant orchestra.

An actor who wants to acquire the science of gesticulation, who wants to learn how to calculate, select and make rhythmic a gesture-language that will harmonise with the spoken language composed by the author, must submit to a training in formation and suppleness.

The attempt to imitate nature by means of the artificial is always stimulating. After all there is no merit in the natural being natural. It is precisely because a violin is hollow like a death-mask that it is so grand to give it a soul. To re-create life is to defy death. Hence creation should set out from that point; we start again but working backwards.

Gesture has its own language just as breathing has. Just as the heart beats the iambic foot (systole, diastole) and just as our breathing breathes the iambic foot (in-breathing, out-breathing) so gesture bases its rhythm on the iambic foot (contraction, decontraction). We proceed iambically.

Just as spoken language has its syntax and metre, so has the language of gesture.

And moreover gesture is narrowly linked to breathing, by the very way that breathing works. For are not the movements of breathing visible? The thoracic cage is a sort of headquarters whither messages are sent, whence orders are hurriedly issued for

Lucien Coutaud: décor for *Le Soulier de Satin*

our conduct about the most trifling matters. The behaviour of the whole man goes flying for a moment to his chest, and the chest 'churns' the slightest things received. Why then should it govern speech and not gesture?

However, we shall not linger over an analysis of our gestures but just say that a solfeggio, an alchemy exists, and every actor should be familiar with it.

And this 'transposed' gesticulation is as removed from ordinary gesticulation as dancing is; just as the alexandrine is as removed from ordinary prose as song is.

Briefly, the stylised, chosen and rhythmic gestures should be exactly similar to the spoken form selected and stylised by the author.

The plastic deportment of the characters should not duplicate what is revealed by the spoken word; it should be complementary to it.

It often happens that we say by word of mouth only what we choose to reveal; but we are given away by our gestures which betray what we hoped to hide. Close observation of gesture is a valuable means by which a psycho-analyst can discover what a person is reluctant to admit.

So at rehearsals a whole plastic language should be minutely worked out. It should constitute to a certain extent a secret, subconscious and subterranean revelation of the action. Conjointly and simultaneously with the spoken word, then, there should be a visible language, reinforcing or contradicting what is said. Buried secrets, bad faith, dissimulation, impulses, weaknesses, evasions . . . closely-observed ways of behaviour that make a kind of undercurrent to the broad official behaviour. Sometimes the Character's movements are influenced by something that has just happened, something that is going to happen, sometimes they are in narrow relation to what is happening; hence the gesticulation can unwedge itself in one direction or another from what is actually being spoken; rather as the colour goes outside the lines in some of the *images d'Épinal*.

Finally *Phèdre* taught me to see a work as a symphony. Just as it amused me to try to probe the scansion of the 1,654 alexandrines of *Phèdre*, so I loved trying to hear the movements of a symphony in the work as a whole.

I have spoken elsewhere of the cruel, permanent and implacable duel which takes place in a work between taste and temperament. Racine's case provides us with the most striking example of this. It is known that when he was writing *Mithridate* in the Tuileries Gardens he used to declaim aloud, and in his ardour so dismayed the gardeners who were tending the flower-beds that they stood by to be ready to help him if need be. They thought he was a desperate man preparing to throw himself into the pool.

The sweet and gentle Racine.

Racine was one of the most brutal monsters and at the same time one of the most civilised artists. But he was always sufficiently robust to hold the monster at bay in the interests of a work of art.

*

Phèdre gave me an insight into the nature of tragedy.

Tragedy is the highest form of dramatic art, not because it is the most difficult to act, nor the most difficult to write, but because it exacts a vitality capable of going beyond the *Instinct for Self-preservation*.

Nothing is more difficult to write than a comedy, because the 'comic' will not tolerate mediocrity, nor even 'averageness'.

I do not mean to imply that tragedy will tolerate mediocrity. Art can never tolerate mediocrity. But whereas an 'average' tragedy is bearable, an 'average' comedy isn't. With comedy it is all or nothing, since it is a quick unlocking and not a slow 'boiling-up'. And the same thing goes for the comic actor. The comic actor is a world that picks out the comic, and this world is either there or not there; work, alas, doesn't make much difference. As I see it, the actor has to undergo a metamorphosis.

Hence comic art is in a way rarer than tragic art; but tragic art is more exhilarating. In tragedy physical beauty and good diction are not the point; the point is whether you are able, or not, to give yourself to the death.

For tragic art begins where the instinct for self-preservation stops. The instinct for self-preservation is the frontier beyond which lies tragedy.

"Grace aux Dieux! Mon malheur passe mon espérance!"

It is the voluptuous relishing of disaster overflowing from an excess of vitality. A sort of defiance of death and the Gods which makes the tragic actor, in the moment of utmost calamity, at his most powerful.

When a tragic character falls he doesn't sink down, he crashes down and flattens himself on the ground. It is his own black will that is fulfilling the work of Destiny. He rivals the Gods with regard to himself. He is at their level. He is in competition with them. In competition with them against himself; through an excess of vitality.

But when the comic character stumbles on the instinct for self-preservation, as if it were a pebble on the road, he stops and retraces his steps while making a pirouette to keep himself in countenance. This is what Jouvet demonstrated so intelligently in *Arnolphe*. Adventure was going to catch up with him. Only a little more, and he would have stepped into tragedy and been a Shakespearean character. But he suddenly saved the situation by a piece of foolery that lowered the temperature almost brutally and thanks to which Arnolphe remains a comic character.

To play tragedy, then, demands such a gift of self that there is no one physically capable of drawing an audience and bringing it to 'white heat'—as has to happen—unless he has recourse to *Rhythm*.

Let me explain what I mean. When one plays comedy, straight drama or tragedy, it is *indispensable* that the CHARACTER should always be SINCERE. It is not indispensable that the actor, who is playing the Character, should be so. While the Character is living truly and sincerely on the stage the actor representing him often has obstacles to cross that prevent him from being whole-heartedly sincere. The actor, especially when he is playing great parts, should have a third eye, for he should be watching not only the unfolding of the action and the behaviour of the Character he is playing, but also the general progress of the performance.

If the play that is being interpreted belongs to a theatre-form that is technically easy, then the actor can give himself up to sincerity side by side with his Character (who will be all the better for it). This is the case in the typical 'boulevard' play.

If on the other hand the play that is being interpreted belongs to a technically difficult theatre-form—such as the classics in general—the actor must forgo a little of his sincerity (like dropping ballast) so as better to supervise what he is doing. Example: Marivaux, Molière.

If, finally, a very difficult and exhausting theatre-form is being interpreted, such as tragedy, in which absolute sincerity would land the actor far beyond the instinct of self-preservation and in a complete destruction of himself, then the actor must have recourse to a sublimated solution: he appeals to Rhythm.

Earlier I was talking about the lyrical state: the expansion of the soul which causes the whole Being to become Rhythm.

I would go so far as to say that it is only by means of Rhythm that the lyrical state can be imparted to the audience.

It is only by means of Rhythm that true tears can be made to flow, the tears that come at the sound of Orpheus' lyre.

It is only through Rhythm that the actor can resist his part physically while laying bare an utterly sincere Character.

In the most simple theatre-forms, comedy or straight drama, the audience can be impressed by great sincerity straight away, by osmosis or direct impregnation. But in tragedy, where death is defied, and where the Character snatches his own destiny from the Gods by a Promethean reaction, the actor cannot possibly sustain his Character right up to the climax of the action unless he reaches the higher plane where everything is Rhythm.

Where there is no rhythm Tragedy is merely theatrical, in the popular sense of the word.

As I plunged deeper into *Phèdre* I found more and more striking corroboration of all that I had hitherto thought about dramatic art:

> the uses of breathing,
> the waking-dream,
> the plastic exercise of the mouth,
> the choice of gesture,
> Rhythm, etc., etc.

My professional study of *Phèdre*, then, enriched my whole being. Technically I made great progress, and I was strengthened morally.

I had approached the theatre along such winding paths that sometimes I found even myself in doubt about my ideas, the more so as Doubt concerning my ideas was widespread in 'normal' theatre circles. So my love and courage were redoubled when I saw that the purest diamond of our classical heritage was confirming my ideas (at least so it seemed to me!).

4

Various Reflections

IT often falls to us to have to give an opinion on Diderot's famous *Paradoxe du Comédien*. There is no more embarrassing question for an actor, because, to begin with, Diderot's *Paradoxe* is one that has to do exclusively with the spectator. Yet nine times out of ten we force ourselves to think up an answer, not wanting to be left behind. But quite frankly I don't think it has ever entered a real actor's head to see his craft in the light of a paradox.

For us actors I think there is no paradox.

Why?

Man is double. At least so it is thought. "I find two men within me," Racine said. In fact everyone finds this. So we come pat on the problem of man and his double. Let us take it as a datum. In man there is a double position: the first one is real, visible, palpable; the second is impalpable, only apprehended, present, yes, but invisible—that is the double.

Yet this other-self, if subjected to intensive and stubborn scrutiny, finally comes out into the open—in two places, or rather in two ways. First of all in the eye.

When we gaze at a human being for a very long time we finally see him as a sort of animal, nerveless, compact in his bony shell, and revealing himself only—by his eyes. Nothing is visible in this animal except the eyes. Each eye is at its window, its socket-window. It looks up and down, it rolls voluptuously. Suddenly it fixes us obliquely, and with a frightening stillness. Then it half-hides itself, bashful. And finally the blind is lowered and it disappears.

We have a feeling that if we had a small two-pronged fork

and placed it briskly under the eye we could scoop this inner-nightmare-animal out from its bony carcase—just as we do with shell-fish. But plucked out or not, nerveless animal or not, it is certain that the eye of man watches us with the air 'of being two'.

The second way in which the other-self is betrayed is by the voice. Supposing we have opposite us a man of medium size, commonplace appearance and wearing mass-produced clothes; suddenly from this average man there comes forth a voice—deep, noble, authoritative, intelligent, sparkling, uttering well-chosen, precise and elegant words. If we close our eyes and perceive this man by his voice alone we imagine him to be a man of stature, elegant and yet powerful—of a chosen race. We open our eyes, and lo! we see someone quite different. By the revelation of the voice, the man is two.

And again from a beautiful and athletic physique, like Greek sculpture, there can issue a pale, little-girl's voice. And so on indefinitely.

Hence the double can be perceived through the eye and the voice.

The Theatre makes use of man's duality not only by its re-creation of life on the stage, but by its very existence.

The theatre, not content with putting double characters on the stage, is in itself a double game.

The human being that it brings to life on the stage is, in fact, *as double as can be*. Both his 'positions' have a name; the first is the *Character* or Part he is playing, real and palpable with a visible presence. The second is the *Actor*, concealed in the bony carcase and showing himself as little as possible.

As in Maelzel's *Le Joueur d'Échec*, discussed by Edgar Allan Poe, it is the *actor*, within, who directs the whole game which the *character*, externally present, gives the appearance of playing.

In order that credibility should be absolute, it is hence indispensable that the Character should be *sincere*; but it is not obligatory that the actor, within, should be so. If the play is straightforward

FÉLIX LABISSE : décor for *The Trial*

123

then the actor can give himself over to sincerity and the character will be all the better for it. But if the play is hard the actor must organise and handle his sincerity with care so as to be prepared to meet the obstacles in his path, or simply so as to hold some of his power in reserve, for though the actor need not himself be sincere it is essential that he should have a *permanent control*, for it is he who governs the Character.

A tragic actor whose acting is highly stylised, who speaks in alexandrines and evolves within a crystallised, complicated but symmetrical situation, who obeys an arithmetical rhythm with both voice and body—this sort of actor must cultivate the faculty of control, for without it he will never carry his Character through to the bitter end.

The more difficult the play the more the actor, behind his Character, should husband his own sincerity, for the risk of the Character being found wanting in 'authenticity' is greater.

The actor's problem, then, lies in the *control of one sincerity*. But this is not a paradox since man is double. It is rather a challenge.

The theatre has built a whole art round the actor, based on 'the man and his double'—the actor and his Character.

And now, why shouldn't we say something about the spectator's paradoxical position? The spectator who, if he too were not made up of 'a man and his double', would be a sheer monster to applaud Nero. It is precisely because he is a dual person that, shocked by Nero, he can applaud de Max.

II MEETING WITH J.-P. SARTRE

I made the acquaintance of J.-P. Sartre in 1941 in connection with his first play, *Les Mouches*. I had already read his *La Nausée* and *Le Mur* and they had at once taken their place among my favourite books, beside the early Faulkners, the early Caldwells, the early Steinbecks, Melville and Malraux. At that time he was beginning to make his way in the theatrical world and we had long enthralling conversations together.

PLATE I

MAURICE BRIANCHON: décor for *Les Fausses Confidences*

PLATE II

Pierre Cabanne: *Baptiste*

Sartre is the prodigious outcome of the inner relationship between what has been given him and what he has made of it. A fine partnership of the left hand with the right. He is a master in the art of making use of his Destiny. If our Destiny cannot be altered, at least we can use it in our own way. There, if I have understood aright, lies the meaning of liberty.

Given the same Destiny one man will make something of it and another man won't. In other words, man is free to make something of his Destiny just as he is free to make nothing of it. Sartre has made a lot of the Destiny affixed to him.

The life of an artisan of the theatre, filled as it is to a great extent with sheer execution, is incomplete and unfertile unless backed up by the creator of the theatre, the *writer*, the author whose rôle it is to provide the theatre-material. The artisan of the theatre whose days are taken up with the tasks of execution is not in a position to go forth and seek the provider. Yet if he has no author behind him his stock empties. Without the author he feels like an orphan. The author is the Father.

So the theatre phenomenon is a ternary, too, a ternary in which the author is the male element, the audience the female element, and the players the neuter element. Each one brings its share of Truth, Purity and Virtue in the pursuit of Perfection. The author, Truth; the audience Purity; the players Virtue.

Sartre is a man who makes you think, liberates you.

> *Judged by their words, all men are the same; it is their deeds that unmask their differences.*
> MOLIÈRE: *L'Avare*

Nothing could have touched me more nearly than his conception of deeds—if only in its theatrical implications. The only thing that counts with man, for our judgment of man, is: his deeds.

The whole conduct of man is a deed, a deed that he performs really on behalf of himself, for his own advantage or protection.

I

Even emotion is a deed, a 'borderline-case' deed.

Unmasking the crime of bad faith in a man; trying to see through a most carefully dissimulated manner; catching hold of gestures, inflections or even answers that give him away in spite of himself; watching him pounce on something of secondary importance so as to gain time with regard to something of major importance: in short laying man bare by observing his 'behaviour', setting out from the principle that consciously or unconsciously no one ever does anything for nothing. That was what preoccupied us, Sartre and myself, in our conversations. And all that leads narrowly and exactly to Poetic Realism.

III CONCERNING EMOTION

Here follow some tentative remarks about deeds in general that may be useful to actors—deeds in general, human behaviour and especially the emotions (all of which Sartre had studied at the philosophical level).

If emotion is a state, the actor should never take cognizance of it. In fact we never can take cognizance of an emotion while we are in its grip, but only when it has passed. Otherwise the emotion disappears. The actor lives uniquely in the present; he is continually jumping from one present to the next. In the course of these successive presents he executes a series of actions which deposit upon him a sort of sweat which is nothing else but the state of emotion. This sweat is to his acting what juice is to fruit. But once he starts perceiving and taking cognizance of his state of emotion, the sweat evaporates forthwith, the emotion disappears and the acting dries up.

There is no actor who can act convincingly with his own genuine emotion. Hence actors who want to play by their emotion are obliged to invent a false one. But the tears produced by nervous tension, the quivering lips and shaking hands do not deceive the qualified audience, the one we should especially try to please.

So we cannot think "I am moved" without at once ceasing to be so. We can say: "I was moved," or rather "I should have been moved."

In the present tense we can only say "he is moved." We can take cognizance only of the emotion of another. Thus to the audience falls the peculiar joy of perceiving and savouring the emotion suffered by the actor. But if the actor, more or less moved himself, is moving, the audience in its turn must not speak or think: it must simply undergo emotion.

Ideally then, no one in a theatre should allude to the fragile phenomenon, emotion. Everyone, both players and audience alike, though under its influence, must concern themselves with actions.

Whether the actor weeps or not is immaterial; the essential thing is that he should cause tears to flow and that no one should stop to think about it.

When the phenomenon of collective emotion in a theatre goes so far as to become unbearable, the audience falls back on a reaction that, by exposing the high temperature of the common emotion, automatically lowers it so that it becomes bearable again: in other words, it claps.

The emotion had been so great, the illusion threatened to be so perfect, that for a moment the audience was lost. Seized with a sort of zealous panic, it claps. For a moment it thought Nero was really there; so, to regain its self-possession, it had to clap de Max. The paradox of the spectator of which we were speaking above.

So it is by applause that the audience protects itself against too strong an emotion.

The fact is that emotion is less a state than a reaction, a defensive reflex. And it is as such that emotion is interesting.

Let us examine the sort of reaction that it is. Any kind of act is a struggle. A struggle implies the existence of two antagonistic forces. When the struggle is nearing its end and one of the two forces is on the point of winning over the other, the latter, at its last gasp, has recourse to a final reaction, a magic reaction that we call: emotion. This reaction usually makes a choice from among four principal metamorphoses:

1. It makes the opposing force disappear as if by magic.
   Or:
2. It artificially transforms the opposing force, preferably in such a way as to diminish its power.
   Or:
3. It makes itself disappear.
   Or:
4. It transforms itself, still magically, and preferably in such a way to make itself seem more dangerous than it really is.

So, by the disappearance or the illusory transformation of the antagonistic force, we believe we can either escape from that force or else vanquish it; just as we think we can escape from it or vanquish it by the disappearance or transformation of ourselves.

Example: I have to cross an unknown and apparently dangerous piece of land. I whistle and proceed in a not-caring kind of way as if 'nothing was up'. In fact I am artificially suppressing the danger.

Suddenly an armed assassin looms up before me: I faint. What I am really doing is making myself disappear.

When I come to I see several policemen trying to bring me round. Their manner seems to suggest a certain contempt for the fear I had felt. That wounds my pride, but is there anything I can do about it? Yes: I become angry and start insulting them. In reality I am making myself more frightening than I really am, I am transforming myself. They become angry in their turn and threaten to arrest me for insulting the police, so then I burst out laughing. What I am really doing is transforming them and metamorphosing them into friends, into 'buddies', and I turn the whole distressing incident into a joke. I magically change the atmosphere.

Once again home, torpor takes hold of me. No one can get a word out of me; I carry on as if I were suffering from amnesia.

Everyone says: "He's sad." But in fact my whole being has gone over to the side of oblivion. I have lived successively: fear, anger, laughter and sadness.

In drama characters behave no differently from this. And the way in which they react when the limit of emotion has been reached gives the most interesting insight into their characters.

The fainting of Lorenzo at the moment of the duel; the cry, "A rat! a rat!" at the moment of Hamlet's murder of Polonius; Phèdre placing the picture of Thésée over that of Hippolyte at the moment of declaration—such things are so many keys that unlock the souls of heroes and heroines.

So definitely the actor shouldn't look on his character's emotions as 'states' (just as he should not think about the sweat beading his body during the performance); but he should attach great importance to emotions seen as 'behaviour', as last-resort actions. If he does this he will be able to convince himself that characters never arrest the action in order needlessly to display their feelings; no, they are continually in action and reaction. They reason, they plead, they argue, they fight with or against others, even with or against themselves. They dispute, answer back, dissimulate, deceive others or themselves with greater or less bad faith; but they never stop.

The audience is at liberty to distinguish between these actions: actions proper, feelings, emotions. For the actor who is right within the drama there is only 'behaviour'.

Only DEEDS.

IV THE THEATRE, THE ART OF ACTUALITY

Again it was with Sartre that I studied Racine's preface to *Bajazet* and got to understand it better. The following passage is very significant:

"I would not advise an author, seeking a subject for a tragedy, to choose a situation as recent as this one of mine, if its events have taken place in the country where he wants his tragedy to be played; nor should I advise him to put heroes on the stage who might be known to the audience. The characters of tragedy should be seen with a different eye from the one we use when looking at people near at hand. . . ." In other words:

"The distance between countries makes up to a certain extent for a too great proximity in time; *for ordinary people make hardly any distinction between what, if I may so put it, lies a thousand years away and what lies a thousand miles away.*"

That touches the core of the problem of the modern theatre.

The art of the Theatre,

because it is ephemeral like the Present;

because theatrical performance, *the only satisfactory manifestation* of the art of the theatre (for the book of a play gives but its bleak quintessence) belongs narrowly to legend and disregards history;

because the art of the theatre deals essentially with the Present and the Simultaneous;

because it grasps, in the interests of its very existence, everything in life that is made up of exchanges, movement and rhythm;

because it is the very art of Becoming, or of the passing moment;

because of all these things,

the art of the theatre is essentially an art of *Actuality*.

When we put on French or foreign classics we are giving ourselves excellent practice and keeping in trim; they nourish our art and through them progress can be made; but they add nothing to the theatrical output of an epoch.

The style of an epoch—whether it be the style of its furniture or its drama—is living only in so far as it is 'actual'. Seventeenth-century theatre will for ever be stamped with the manners of Louis XIV's court. Eighteenth-century theatre will live because of its 'topical' introduction of the bourgeoisie (*Les Fausses Confidences*). Example: "The altercation between Madame Argente's daughter and Monsieur le Comte" in which social questions rear their head such as: "A steward's *position*! That's delicious!" "Why shouldn't he have a position?"

Shakespeare's plays are imbued with the reign of Queen

Elizabeth. Aristophanes and Plautus are concerned with their contemporaries; Musset smacks of his epoch and so does Becque.

Thus our generation will produce something of theatrical validity only if that thing is inspired by the 'Actual'.

But what sort of thing can the Actual inspire?

Our epoch is an epoch of transition. We are living between two eras, two streams. One of them is related to the Past, to the near tradition, and it binds us to the great bourgeois epoch whose close we sometimes seem to be living. The other links us to the Future, beyond the anguish of expectation and the tragic times we have already seen, and gives us a presentiment of a further period of unrest. We are tossed between drama and tragedy, both seasoned with the absurd.

If our present-day theatrical production lacks co-ordination and seems to have several styles it is precisely because our epoch is hesitating between two styles, between two conceptions of life. On the one hand there is the desire to prolong our traditional way of life as long as possible, and on the other the urge to break with the past and usher in a new, still ill-defined way of life. In the field of drama this gives us:

On the one hand the continuation of the bourgeois theatre, the flourishing of the 'boulevard' type of play; and on the other hand experiments that go in the dead opposite direction, towards new forms as yet barely defined.

To these two styles we must add two more, both belonging to the *escapism* caused by the anguish our epoch specialises in. In the first of these the escape is into the past: Gaston Baty into the 1840's, Montherlant into the Italian Renaissance, etc. In the second the escape lies through the imagination (as in certain of Audiberti's plays).

Faced with the Actual, then, artists respond in various ways. Some have a legitimate nostalgia for the past, they prefer to observe our epoch with the intelligent, wise, perspicacious and refined eye of our fathers. Others are curious about the Future and would like already to be in tune with an epoch whose outline is not yet clear. Others, again, *escape*—either by means of magically wafting themselves into an epoch of their own choice, or else by giving free rein to their imagination.

But there is a serious difficulty inseparable from considerations about the desirability of treating 'actual' subjects in the theatre. And Racine was the first to put his finger on it:

"A subject chosen from an epoch too near to our own, whether in time or place, cannot inspire our respect."

Strictly speaking such a subject can only succeed if treated satirically. For all grandeur is summarily excluded from a subject too near to ourselves in time or place.

"Our respect for heroes increases in proportion as they are removed from us", Racine said in his preface to *Bajazet: major e longinquo reverentia*.

However, none of the rules governing the dramatic poem makes mention of this, as Racine pointed out, and that was why he did not give up his *Bajazet* venture. Nevertheless the fact remains.

If the spectator is to throw himself utterly into the action of a play and abandon himself to fear or compassion, then there must from the outset be: distance.

Distance can be created by the intermediary of Time. This is how Sartre does it in *Les Mouches* and Giraudoux in *La Guerre de Troie*. In fact it is the most usual expedient.

In *Antony and Cleopatra* there is a description of Caesar and Mark Antony:

> Then, world, thou hast a pair of chaps, no more;
> And throw between them all the food thou hast,
> They'll grind the one the other.

Now I am at perfect liberty when I hear this to think of the Russians and the Americans. But if I were to say that phrase on the stage, substituting Truman and Stalin for Caesar and Mark Antony . . . it just couldn't be said on the stage.

Distance by means of Time makes the topical idea possible.

Distance can also be created by the intermediary of *Space*, whether it be Papua or some imaginary country.

When we started our inquiry we hadn't intended to go beyond these laws of distance. Yet we can't help asking ourselves whether distance can be evoked by subterfuges other than those of Time and Space.

The answer is, yes. It can be evoked by *Technique*.

Distance by means of technique already exists in the cinema. The image, replacing the flesh-and-blood presence of the actor, in itself constitutes distance. At all events topicality is much more bearable in the cinema than on the stage.

Hence, the ways in which to create distance so as to make a topical subject 'respect-able' are:

> by Time,
> Space
> and TECHNIQUE.

And that led me back to the mass of preoccupations that had been haunting me ever since *Hunger*, preoccupations that life at the Français had not effaced and that the preface to *Bajazet*, among other things, had reawakened.

"The overhauling of the technical palette of the actor."

Now that the art of the cinema has, rightly, made its own all that was documentary in dramatic art—even the Freudian document, even the dream,

dramatic art, as it is played out on the stage, must undergo a revolution. And the revolution will be a technical revolution. An overhauling of the actor's technique.

But just as the technique of certain instruments must have come into being through the demands of the composer who suddenly needed them to do new things, so the actor's technique depends for its modification on the demands of the author.

The artisan of the theatre can tear his hair and walk round in circles, as in dreams; the fact remains that the fate of theatrical art lies exclusively in the hands of the author.

Jean Louis Barrault et Pierre Renoir

PIERRE CABANNE: Jean-Louis Barrault and Pierre Renoir in *Hamlet*

134

May I give one or two examples of one sort of technique that will transmit the shock of distance to the audience? the things an actor should do to create a special world that the audience will feel to be as far removed from this world as Time and Space would make it?

In my chapter about *Hunger* I referred to a sort of double game that the actor had to play. On the one hand the part proper of the character he was interpreting, and on the other hand a sort of underlying part conveying the type of theatre the play belonged to. He had to play the part of the setting, of the décor, so that the audience should be in no doubt about the unfolding of the action in spite of the fact that no object or material décor was there to throw light on it.

It was this second part, the underlying one, that gave the audience the illusion of a world far removed from its customary one and that thus provided the requisite impact of distance.

It is in *Hunger* and Kafka's *Trial* that examples are to be found: going up steps, the captain's mask, comings and goings in the street, scenes of *fatrasie* (*Hunger*). The disappearance of sections of the décor during the action; simultaneous scene of the Bank, the lawyer's bed, the great judge's picture, the kitchen and the street; the danced execution-march, the execution ballet with the knife, the nightmarish walks down the corridors of the law courts, etc., etc. (*The Trial*).

But *Hunger* and *The Trial* are 'personal' plays. Consequently they do not bring conclusive proof.

Some authors have already applied themselves to the problem of distance, of distance by means of *technique*.

For example Salacrou, particularly in *L'Inconnu d'Arras* and *Les Nuits de la Colère* where he made the living, the dead and the dying have a conversation together! Distance, too, when he goes back in time or breaks the chronological order of time.

Obey, too, suggests remoteness by means of technique. And Claudel's special way of writing, among all its other virtues, surely has that of producing distance.

V   THE THEATRE, THE ART OF JUSTICE

> *Creon: The same fate should not be meted out*
> *to the just man and the criminal.*
> *Antigone: We do not know whether these rules*
> *are sacred among the dead.*
>
> SOPHOCLES
>
> *Excesses should be stamped out before fires.*
>
> HERACLITUS

Our conversations which, like cranking-up, started me thinking so much about my art (and on which the foregoing commentary is by now all my own and does not involve J.-P. Sartre) also covered the question of the *social import of the theatre*. And we quite naturally came to the following conclusion:

That the art of the theatre is essentially an *art of Justice*.

Aristotle said that if tragedy wanted to preserve its greatness it must rest on *State reasons*.

We shall say in a more general way that all subjects are dramatic if they pose *questions concerning rights*.

The theatre is a place where, in a crystallised form, opposing forces confront each other. In the course of the conflict thus created each of these forces pleads its own rights, each thinks itself to be in the right and wants to get the upper hand.

In fact at the theatre we are always assisting at a vast *settling of accounts*. From all the opposing rights, from the Rugby scrum of rights, there should by degrees emerge a Sentence. Justice. And the spectator isn't satisfied unless the sentence is just.

Just, not in relation to the individuals participating in the conflict, but in relation to Life, in the universal sense of the word. And what is the just life? It is the balanced life. As soon as the word 'just' rises above the level of men, its true sense and its figurative sense melt into each other and *justice* becomes equivalent to *justness*.

Life is a tight-rope dancer making his way along a rope and in continual danger of losing his balance, continual danger of death.

Only measure, justness . . . justice, re-establishes and maintains the balance of life.

As for man within life, he is always more or less cleft in two. Man sins through *excess*. In his desire to indulge his passions, he tends to upset the equilibrium.

Man's passions rise up and face each other—conflict is born—and conflict degenerates into the Rugby scrum we were talking about just now. The balance of life is threatened. Threatened even with Death, were it not for the Sentence emerging from the scrum, the SPIRIT OF JUSTICE that re-establishes the equilibrium. Life has become just again: justness, justice.

In the course of the bitter conflict some ballast has been dropped overboard. This ballast is the victims who are also sometimes the heroes.

At the conclusion of a well-conducted dramatic conflict, life should not only be *righted*, but *fortified*. The place has been *cleaned up* and anyone who has made the conflict his own throughout the evening finds that he too is cleansed, righted, revivified. That is what justice does: it cleans, rightens, revivifies.

And this is what the audience subconsciously comes to find; it comes to live through a series of adventures that will remove a mass of its own problems of conscience, problems that could not be properly settled except in the light of the purer spirit of justice.

The theatre is the art of justice.

There lies the social rôle of the theatre.

In the sight of the Gods, and after the oaths he has taken and broken, it is just that Hippolyte should die.

It is just that Hamlet should be killed, in the sight of Life; and just too that Fortinbras should wind everything up.

Always make sure that the universal spirit of justice has been respected in a play. If not: beware of the mood of the audience. The theme of *The Trial* was at once the most theatrical and the most thorny since it called in question precisely this universal justice by taking up the dossier of original sin!

Once the spirit of justice is respected, everything is permissible.

Sartre was obviously thinking of this when he wrote *Huis Clos*. In *Huis Clos* there is nothing to be said, the characters are in hell! JUSTICE.

5

Le Soulier de Satin

I OWE one of my keenest theatre joys to Jean-Louis Vaudoyer, for it was he who made it possible for us to put *Le Soulier de Satin* on at the Français.

Without his solid backing and unfailing confidence in me the *Soulier* might never have known the lustre of those footlights.

After countless set-backs and more than eighteen months' hard work, the *Soulier* was finally played for the first time on 23 November, 1943.

I shall quote from an article I wrote about it in the April, 1944, issue of a Swiss review, *Formes et Couleurs*:

> The play, *Le Soulier de Satin*, is the most representative of Paul Claudel's dramatic genius, forming, so to speak, its synthesis. *L'Arbre* (and particularly *Tête d'Or*), *Partage de Midi*, *L'Annonce*, *L'Otage*, and even *Protée* send forth ramifications all of which we meet again in *Le Soulier de Satin*. And even the *Livre de Christophe Colomb*, written after the *Soulier*, is surely too a magnificent throw-back to the life of the conquistador, Rodrigue de Manacor.
>
> Each of these plays, whichever of the poet's "styles" it belongs to, bears on *Le Soulier de Satin* in its own peculiar way.
>
> Hence for anyone whose appetite has been whetted by Paul Claudel's art, the race between *Tête d'Or*, *Partage de Midi*, *Le Soulier*, and *Christophe Colomb* will naturally be won by the Rodrigue-Prouhèze team. It is simply a matter of eating first what one likes best. Greed.

However, pouncing on *Le Soulier de Satin* and holding it tight in our arms meant embarking on a close fight with the entire machinery of the theatre. We had to weld our talented actors into a whole (and it is often to be remarked that the more talented the actor the harder he is to weld!), we had to find a satisfactory setting, a team of accomplished technicians and clever collaborators on the artistic side.

But the encouragement, help and protection of Jean-Louis Vaudoyer, the Administrator of the Comédie Française, made all these things possible; and thanks to the perceptiveness of the Reading Committee the play was accepted. So I had at my disposal the best possible stage, an outstanding staff and an excellent company. Honegger and Lucien Coutaud, whom I sounded, joined us with enthusiasm. So all that remained was to win over that man of genius, the author.

Our few conversations together had proved to Paul Claudel and myself that our points of view were similar down to the last detail (allowing, of course, for his knowledge as against my ignorance, his experience as against nothing but my wild enthusiasm). We spoke the same language from the very first moment—whether we were discussing the art of gesture, the dramatic importance of breath, or the value of the word and its specifically theatrical composition.

And so I again made my way to Claudel's country home, my plans in my pocket, my inseparable rucksack on my back, and armed with the Administrator's and the Reading Committee's consent; and there I found the master. My proposals were agreeable to him. We worked out the principal modifications together and to my delight he gave me a free hand for the rest. . . .

Eighteen months went by, and it was only after periods of fever, enthusiasm, anxiety, despair, rage and finally sheer grit that *Le Soulier de Satin* at last appeared 'in the flesh'.

It would be both childish and untrue to pretend that *Le Soulier de Satin* first appealed to me by its form. No; it was the play's sheer power and the elevation of its subject that had held me for so many years. But just as a woman whom one is all set to love deeply can suddenly reveal her charm by a detail, as slight as it is

unexpected—a special smile, a wonderfully slender neck, a fore-
arm rounded like a little hot loaf, a delicate foot, an exquisite ear—
so it was a detail that made the play utterly irresistible to me.
Everyone knows that the action takes place largely at sea. The
necessity of catching the motions of the sea was the detail that
excited me. Indeed I began my study of this difficult play with
the scene in which Dona Sept Épées and La Bouchère (the Fourth
Day) are swimming in the rippling sea, a scene that the author
closes with the simple direction: "Here La Bouchère drowns. . . ."
By an irony of fate we had to cut this scene later as the play
exceeded the allotted time.

But *Le Soulier de Satin*, from the point of view of form—
which grips one more and more the further one penetrates into
an art—presented many other problems that had previously just
crossed my path.

To Baudelaire the theatre seemed a meeting-place of the arts,
but nowadays it has become a positive conspiracy of the arts.
The plastic, literary and musical arts all conspire to invade our
stage and enslave the actor. Now *Le Soulier de Satin* is played out
in a large number of different places (we managed to *reduce* the
sets to thirty-three!) and this made great demands on décor.
There had to be music, too, while the whole thing really centres
on Gesture and the spoken Word—and this presented the most
fascinating problems. It closed paths that had already been
explored and opened up new ones. At one point the décor had to
disappear almost as soon as it was put up, had to vanish so as to
become nothing but its imprint on the audience's mind. The
transition, the famous passing moment—so difficult to catch hold
of—from a gesture to a cry, from a phrase to the drawing of a
curtain, from an effect of lighting to a musical overtone, the
passing moment became the major difficulty.

We studied the play with Arthur Honegger who has the
simplicity and humility of all great men, and he ceased to be a
composer only and became a man of the theatre. How many
musicians could boast of such adaptability? It was as a man of the

PLATE III

Jean Denis Malclès: sketch for *Occupe-toi Amélie*

PLATE IV

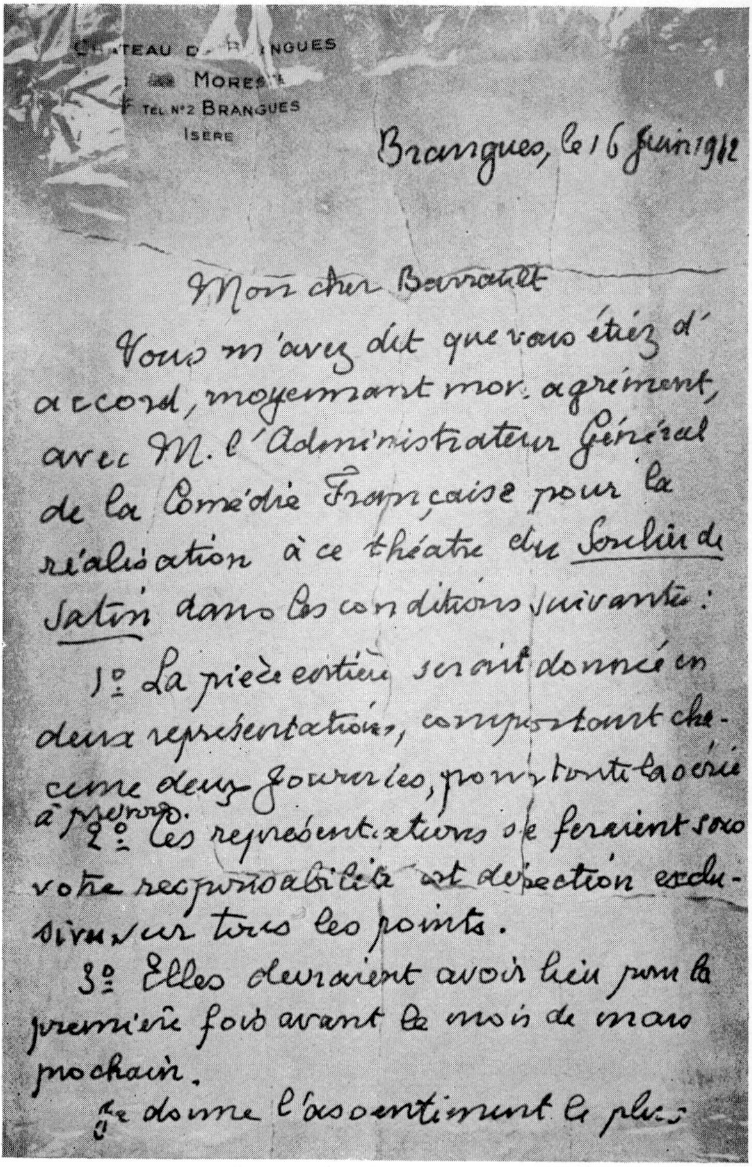

CHATEAU DE BRANGUES
MORESTEL
TEL. N° 2 BRANGUES
ISÈRE

Brangues, le 16 Juin 1942

Mon cher Barrault

Vous m'avez dit que vous étiez d'accord, moyennant mon agrément, avec M. l'Administrateur Général de la Comédie Française pour la réalisation à ce théâtre du Soulier de Satin dans les conditions suivantes:

1° La pièce entière serait donnée en deux représentations, comportant chacune deux journées, pour toute la série à prévoir.

2° Les représentations se feraient sous votre responsabilité et direction exclusives sur tous les points.

3° Elles devraient avoir lieu pour la première fois avant le mois de mars prochain.

Je donne l'assentiment le plus

The letter from Paul Claudel

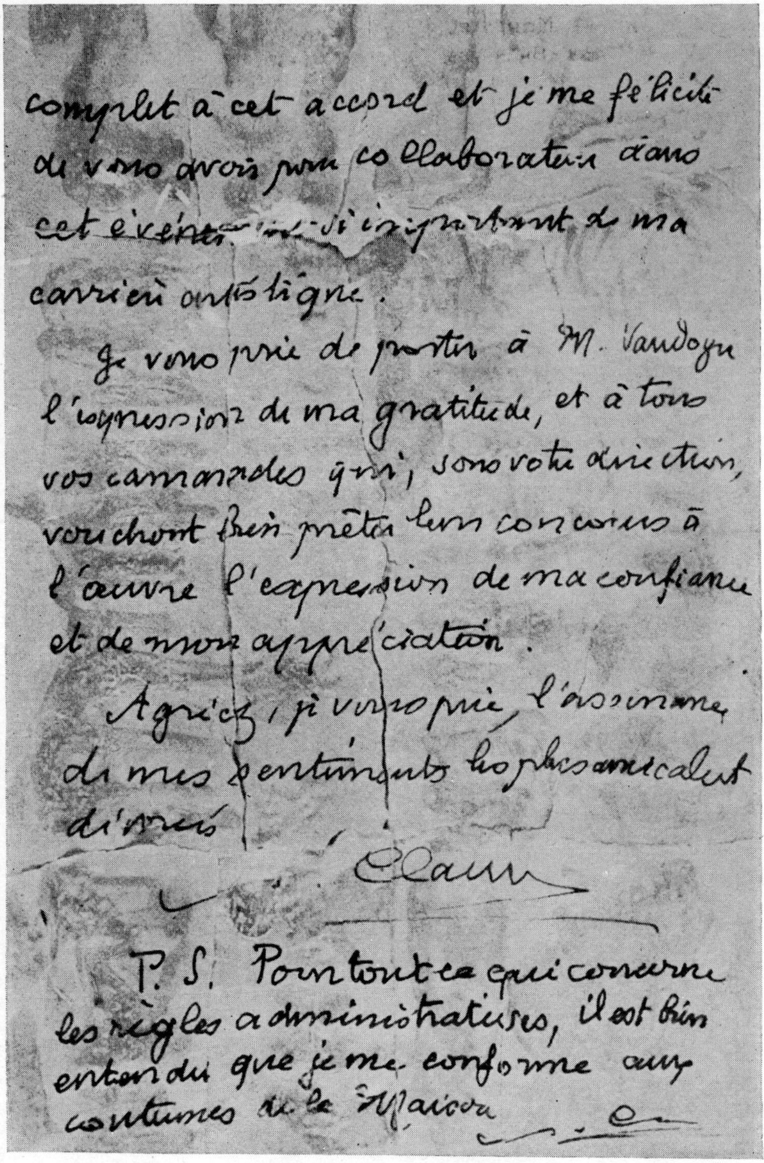

PLATE V

complet à cet accord et je me félicite
de vous avoir pour co collaborateur dans
cet événement si important de ma
carrière artistique.

Je vous prie de porter à M. Vaudoyer
l'expression de ma gratitude, et à tous
vos camarades qui, sous votre direction,
voudront bien prêter leur concours à
l'œuvre l'expression de ma confiance
et de mon appréciation.

Agréez, je vous prie, l'assurance
de mes sentiments les plus amicalest
dévoués

P. Claudel

P. S. Pour tout ce qui concerne
les règles administratives, il est bien
entendu que je me conforme aux
coutumes de la Maison.

The letter from Paul Claudel

PLATE VI

ANDRÉ MASSON: The Ghost, *Hamlet*

theatre that Honegger composed *Noise* and clothed *Silence*. At
no moment was his participation in the enterprise that of a
'one-horse' man. He contrived to put his music at the service of
theatre and never expected it to occupy unrightfully the stage.
And the peculiar unity that emerged from a spectacle so complex
was due in great measure to Honegger's flexibility. Lucien
Coutaud, too, proved himself a theatre man and not merely a
painter cluttering up the stage. He managed with remarkable
brilliance to adapt himself to the exacting demands of the production as a whole. Sets and costumes should not be loud, they
should be exact and should strike the right note. In perfect
concord we three friends laid ourselves at the service of the work.
And the company of the Français on its side—its interest swiftly
won over by the problems of mime and diction, the 'breathed'
character of Claudel's prose-poetry, the chargedness of his words,
his 'intelligible mouthfuls', the humanly exact rhythm (like
pulsation) of his lines based principally on the iambic and the
anapaest—the admirable company of the Français throughout the
whole work showed a docility such as is met with only among
great professionals.

But the Entity that was to bring the ultimate chord to this
human symphony was the Public—whose evolution is really
remarkable.

The first condition that a good production (whether of the
cinema or the theatre) should fulfil is that it should pass by
unobserved; but when there are innovations appearing for the
first time or seldom made use of before there is an exception—for
it is custom that makes the rule. Every innovation surprises the
public. If the innovation pleases the public, then the public accepts
it and by degrees becomes accustomed to it; the innovation then
becomes the Rule. The theatre is governed by the totality of these
rules and customs. They are called: conventions. At the three taps
the audience falls silent; while the action is unfolding they see
without turning a hair the shadowy outline of the conductor
looming up in front of the stage; when an actor drinks, the glass

is—empty; very often he speaks in a ceilingless room quite by himself; and at the end of the play Hamlet, Othello, Desdemona, all come to life and bow with great ceremony to an audience which, in its turn, shows its admiration by clapping with its 'fore-paws'. All this is custom, the rules of the Game, convention.

But if one wants to inaugurate a new convention, then surprise takes hold of the audience which immediately divides itself into two camps—those 'for' and those 'against'. The conventions of the theatre are in continual evolution. We only have to recall the fluctuations that the Rule of the Three Unities has undergone. The changes of locality that shocked seventeenth-century audiences seem quite normal to us now. Conventions admitted by Oriental audiences (the servants, for instance, who follow the actor about on the stage throughout the whole action) would cool off a Western audience!

For some years now there have been attempts—by means of experiment and research—to increase the number of theatrical conventions, to improve upon the rules of this magnificent Game. They are the innovations of the avant-garde. These attempts have many detractors. And if they are superficial, mere 'plating', as it were, they cannot hold and finally they die. But if one of them 'takes' (rather as the Cordon Bleu says that mayonnaise 'takes'), then provided that it springs from the true art of the theatre a new convention is born and will soon be generally accepted.

Le Soulier de Satin, put on at the Comédie Française, is a proof that the public of to-day has accepted some of the new conventions, for not only did they not shock, but they passed over so to speak unobserved. No attention was drawn to them, either by clapping or disapproval. They were accepted quite naturally and therein lies the great progress that the enterprise brought to light. The motions of the Sea traced in Space by human beings, a wreck floating among the waves represented by a masked actor, boats of all sizes continually breaking away from the human scale, the moon-character describing its 'quarters', the Guardian

Angel's invisible thread 'hooking' Dona Prouhèze, a man on horse-back symbolised by a horse's head, the angle-changes of the sets, etc., etc.; these were some of the means, seldom used hitherto, that seemed to get by quite naturally.

Progress.

Le Soulier de Satin at the Comédie Française showed that the French public were prepared to accept a larger field of expression and to give rein henceforth to its imagination. The theatre casts off more and more material difficulties, replacing them by more perfected 'play'.

Henceforward we can count on these new conventions; and things against which detractors rose up some years ago, and sometimes do still, are accepted by a public capable of evolving.

Victory!

If truth be told the task was sometimes very strenuous.

My first proposal to Paul Claudel was an adaptation of the *Soulier* in two straightforward performances each lasting about three hours. One vast performance in two episodes, the whole lasting about six hours.

It was this first proposal that he accepted when I went to find him at Brangues, rucksack on my back, early in the June of 1942. The letter he wrote for me is shown in Plates IV and V. It was his official permission to go ahead, but it was written under the guise of a personal letter to me so that there would be no difficulties in crossing the line of demarcation at Tournus.

But as luck would have it I was searched at the line of demarcation and the German found the letter. Seized with sudden rage he tore 'my letter' into fragments which he strewed along the corridor. I waited for the train to go and then picked them up. I pieced them together and stuck them on to a sheet of cellophane.

Imagine the equivalent in the seventeenth century. Corneille writing a letter in which he gives the Hôtel de Bourgogne permission to produce the *Cid*. The letter is torn up by the enemy and put together again in its entirety.

The reading of this version before the committee took place at two sittings. The first for the first performance which was accepted with unanimity except for one voice; the second for the second which was turned down.

I had to start all over again. I took it upon myself to make some slight alterations, and finally the committee agreed on an adaptation of the play in one performance so long as it would last only from four and a half to five hours all told, and not exceed the usual time-limit further than that.

Off I went to Brangues again and pleaded with Claudel who finally gave his consent. So then there was another reading to the committee!—for formality's sake—and in this version *Le Soulier de Satin* was accepted.

There followed an intensive correspondence between myself and the author on interzonal post-cards about the choice of who should be in charge of the décor. Coutaud was approved. As for Honegger we were all three in agreement from the start.

I set off for Brangues yet again and played the whole thing through before Claudel. We came to an understanding about the décors, about the detailed spirit of the production, about the various facets of the action, about nuances of diction and even about the pronunciation of certain words.

We worked closely at the prosody of the whole play, and 'armed with all this information' I came back to Paris with the affectionate assurance from Paul Claudel that, as for the rest, I might get ahead as best I could right up to the final rehearsals.

Three times rehearsing started and three times we were dashed against external obstacles. Happily, remembering the experience with Desnos, I had organised my expenditure and ordered the sets and costumes at the start. Without this foresight, perhaps on a certain day that I am not likely to forget . . . our fine project would have had to be abandoned!

Let us bear in mind that we were right in the middle of the Occupation, and that in some quarters our project was not smiled on. The slowness with which we were obliged to work had already caused sarcastic comment in some of the papers. We were waiting, they said, for Eisenhower's arrival to put on Claudel's play, etc., etc.

We needed desperate tenacity to "override the objections", as Péguy said.

The dress rehearsal was ten days off when Claudel arrived in Paris. How scared I was to play the piece through in front of him! The first part lasted two and a half hours without the curtain falling once. This first part went without a hitch. Then there was an interval of ten minutes during which I went and found Claudel, quaking with apprehension.

He said: "They'll get their money's worth all right."

"Anything else?"

"It's all right, it's all right."

I did not press him to say more for it was in the second part that there was our famous 'hurdle'.

I had never been able, in the great scene of the stern-castle, either to get the scene properly placed or to learn the text, and neither had Marie Bell. At this point the play kicked. It had come to life and at this point there was an adhesion. It resisted.

It was because of this that I realised that when one produces a play the author and the producer do not have things all their own way. No, the play itself becomes a third person, standing on its rights, dictating its will. And this person is the most exacting and implacable of the three.

So we went ahead with the rehearsal and everything went well until the stern-castle where, as usual, we stumbled—full stop— discussion. I even dared to suggest a cut.

Claudel said: "Skip that for now and go on to the end."

The rest passed off just as usual. This second part lasted one and three-quarter hours. With the interval the whole thing lasted four and three-quarter hours.

Alone together, Claudel and I recapitulated. We tried to see the whole thing clearly. He said: "It's quite obvious that there is something wrong at that point. I haven't understood a word you've been saying, but let's try to avoid a cut. Before removing the tooth let's try to mend it."

We reviewed the action yet again. The Jesuit Father at the beginning of the play who gives such impetus to the action at the moment of the wreck (Second Day) could, I suggested, somehow intervene again in the second part. That was all Claudel needed; he suddenly disappeared.

The next day I was at the Français at eight o'clock. There was a telephone call for me. Claudel, under the inspiration of the moment, had spent the night re-writing the whole scene. He came and joined me towards nine o'clock still in tears. This man of seventy-six was crying as one cries at eighteen. "It was wonderful," he said, "the whole thing was dictated to me." The gift! We shut ourselves up in a little room in the theatre and he read me what he had written straight off in the night.

Instead of the painting of St. James on the bulkhead, he had substituted a cross made from the fragments of wreckage of the Jesuit Father's boat. Hence, the presence of the Jesuit Father. The whole play was rounded off. Claudel had found the solution.

When I witnessed such swift action, such sureness of touch, I began to regret that Paul Claudel had not devoted his life to being a dramatic author. What a prodigious *théâtre* he would have manufactured!

Indeed I have always recognised his keen sense of true theatre. The stage inspires him and nine times out of ten it is he who is right, even against us.

He never hesitates to sacrifice what he has written—like all creative artists who have a large reserve of imagination; he does not attach a superstitious importance to what is already written.

The next day, with this new version, the scene simply placed itself; Marie Bell and the rest of us learnt our new lines in record time and the whole play became clearer as if by magic.

What joy to work with a man like that! How often have I regretted that we did not meet forty years earlier!

Paul Claudel must have had an enormous influence on my

formation. Paul Claudel is a monument. He is not just a mountain; no, he is the whole round ball of the earth bowling its work-a-day way within the infinite universe of God.

I am still much too much in his thrall to be able to talk about him freely.

And yet what a lot of memories already !

With *Le Soulier de Satin* I realised again my dream of *total theatre*, this time in the service of a really great play.

6

Reforms of the Comédie Française

IN September, 1945, we went at last for a few days' rest in Normandy. One day I went shooting ducks with a gun the village carpenter kindly lent me. We came back drenched to the skin and covered with marsh mud, complete with two teal that my guide had shot.

There, waiting for me, was the Minister's car. Jean de Beer, an old acquaintance of mine and assistant to André Obey, the new Administrator of the Comédie Française, had come charged with the mission of fetching me away.

At the Minister's orders I was to go to Brussels and put on *Le Soulier de Satin* within eight days.

I came back to Paris, the whole company was summoned, and we set out in lorries.

The whole company was there and within three days we put on *Le Soulier de Satin* at the Théâtre de la Monnaie in Brussels.

We gave two gala performances. *Le Soulier de Satin*, written by Claudel, who had been our ambassador in Belgium for many years, marked the brotherly 'coming together again' of the two countries after five years of grim ordeals and separation.

Its success burst out of the confines of the theatre. Windows were broken, and the Belgians sang the two national anthems, theirs and ours, at the tops of their voices. We returned to Paris, our hearts full, still dizzy with the sort of human contact that happens too seldom in life.

I look on those two performances in Brussels as the swan-song of that portion of my life that I was to share with the Comédie Française.

The remainder of the year was sterile, passed in feverish discussions, not to say quarrels.

We made some mistakes. We had good reason. But where was Reason? That, I cannot answer.

Time has flown since those days. The unhappy period is far enough away for me to be able to think about it dispassionately, without reopening any wounds.

Here, in short, is what I sincerely believe I saw and lived through. Here at least is what I understood of the whole business.

"Heavens, what am I going to say to him, and where am I going to begin?"

When I signed on 'for life' with the Société des Comédiens Français I sincerely believed that the society was a private society, economically under-age, yes, but with a spirit sufficiently united to guarantee a certain artistic independence. The Société des Comédiens Français, as I saw it, was rendered under-age, or dependent, on account of the contract it had taken on. This contract consisted in preserving, maintaining and causing to prosper the repertory of the French National Theatre and in serving the spoken French language; in return for which the government granted it a building free—the Théâtre Français—and a subsidy.

Most certainly in the course of its history it had undergone fluctuations; there had been 'highs', there had been 'lows'; but none the less it had remained what I thought it was—a private society. And I knew it to be capable of acts of independence. I could recall such acts in the course of its history. For example:

1. In Le Kain's time the Superintendent of Plays, through the Administrator, wanted to eliminate the corps de ballet at the Français (for at that time the Société des Comédiens Français had a corps de ballet). This decision was not in accord with the wishes of the Comédiens Français, who thus decided to close their theatre. So the corps de ballet was kept.

2. One day Mounet-Sully met Claretie, the then Administrator of the Comédie Française, at the door of the Française, both entering at the same moment. There was an exchange of politeness:

"Pray go in, my dear Administrator."

"No, no, my dear Mounet, you first."

"After you."

"No, after you," etc., etc.

and finally Mounet said to Claretie:

"Pray go in first, my dear Administrator; after all you are *my guest*!"

The spiritual independence of the Société des Comédiens Français could have been safeguarded, it seems to me, so long as the economic life of the Society could balance its budget independently of the subsidy.

And in fact up till the first world war the budget of the Society was balanced independently of the subsidy. The subsidy came into operation only to recoup the expenses involved by the *contract*, that is to say the upkeep of French repertory.

From 1910 to 1914 the budget started not to balance itself. The private Société des Comédiens Français hence showed an annual deficit and the subsidy was necessary to refloat it. And so it became dependent.

Everyone knows that spiritual independence in the present-day organisation of the world depends, alas, on economic independence.

The Société des Comédiens Français, in losing its economic independence, lost by degrees its spiritual independence, to the profit of the people who were floating the Society, that is to say, to the profit of the Minister and therefore the Administrator.

The result being that, since about 1920, the powers of the moral ego of the Société des Comédiens Français have progressively waned, to the advantage of the Minister represented by his Administrator, whose powers have waxed.

The result was great perturbation of mind.

First of all inside the Society itself. Some of the *sociétaires* had

Félix Labisse: décor for *Partage de Midi*

151

a nostalgia for the old independence. Others, on the other hand, settled down comfortably under the disappearance of the responsibility always entailed by independence. Let us call these the civil-service *sociétaires*, or rather the civil-service monks. Others again preferred the passing of power into the hands of one man. They preferred authority and discipline to rather risky independence. They were the military monks.

So there were at least three sorts of *sociétaires*. Which meant that the society had lost its spiritual unity. Fanatical monks, civil-service monks and military monks.

The Comédie Française went well or badly according to whether the Administrator was good or bad. Progress was so-so if the Administrator was middling, but a good diplomat knowing how to hold his job.

It went off the rails in an alarming way when Administrators succeeded one another at a sharp pace, so that at the end of a certain period one could have echoed Louis XVIII's remark about the "*administrateur introuvable*".

It was at this point that the Société des Comédiens Français had arrived in September, 1945. We had become monks without a God.

We pulled the alarm signal.

Everyone knows that if we pull the alarm signal without valid cause we are exposed to a heavy fine.

The Minister who was functioning at that time belonged to the military-Pope category. He summoned us to his presence, lectured us soundly and sent us curtly back to 'barracks' doubtless to see 'if he was there'.[1]

For some time the Minister had evidently forgotten that the Société des Comédiens Français was a private society and not a State theatre. Otherwise how could an 'artist' worthy of the name have endured to bind himself for life to a life so changeable?

---

[1] This is a reference to nursery jargon. The French mother, when exasperated by her child's importunities, sends him trotting off to another room: "to see if I'm there." (Tr.)

When the permanent unity of spirit of the Société des Comédiens Français was suppressed, the life-sentence became a positive renunciation of self.

The Minister then set up a commission whose task it was to draw up anew the constitution of the Société des Comédiens Français. He got people to sit on the commission who had nothing to do with the Société des Comédiens Français. Eminent people yes, but people who were enjoying a private and independent life. The Minister completed the commission by arbitrarily nominating two *sociétaires* of the Comédie Française and one *sociétaire* newly retired.

Not only had the Minister evidently forgotten that the Société des Comédiens Français was a private society, but, alas, some of the *sociétaires* seemed to have forgotten it too. And the disorder into which we had been plunged, as I said before, had unfortunately divided us.

Had we been united we could have insisted that the Minister let the Society be represented on the commission by someone *elected by us*, someone who would be free to reject the findings of the commission.

Had this happened it would have been a striking proof that the Société des Comédiens Français still deserved to be a private society.

But it didn't happen, that's all.

The Comédiens Français agreed passively to submit to the decisions of the commission provided that the possibility of renewing contracts or otherwise was left open for a fortnight.

The eminent people on the commission drew up a new constitution with great conscientiousness, according to which the Comédiens Français could engage themselves again *for life*; and once their labours were over these eminent people returned to their homes and to their precious independent private lives.

There were some of us who didn't want to 'take the veil' a second time unless we could choose our religion ourselves.

The dissenting monk was born.

The reform commission thought it was acting rightly;
those who remained thought they were acting rightly;
we thought we were doing right in leaving.

This crisis made me see that the Société des Comédiens Français was not as private and spiritually independent as I had at first believed.

I had made a mistake.

My destiny once again tipped the scale. Once again I obeyed my destiny. I had just lived for exactly six years in the bosom of the Comédie Française. Six of the most fruitful possible years. The wishes that I had expressed during that walk at Miramont de Quercy with my friend Planson had been strangely granted.

In spite of everything it was with a deep pang that I left, for I had loved with my innermost self the *idea* that I had built up of the Société des Comédiens Français, and I knew full well that I would have a scar FOR LIFE. A scar that would hurt from time to time.

1

Reflections (*continued*)

BEFORE returning to action here are a few more pages of technical observations written with the sole aim of getting them off my chest. Like when one unloads ballast in full flight so as to be lighter.

I CONCERNING MIME AND DANCE

A theatre stage has always made me think of a conjurer's box. A theatre stage has always made me think of a mysterious cube, ten metres a side, a sort of dark room where enchantment reigns.

Let us imagine it: the box, the magic room, the cube.

At the moment it is empty. A block of frozen silence, full of potentialities.

Suddenly there is a squall of noise, a sonorous whirlwind. A breath of music has penetrated there and it turns and turns, up and up, its spirals getting smaller and smaller, like a column of smoke. And from the ground we see a little pyramid of dust rising, turning, whirling round, too, like a top—a potter's wheel gone mad. This little pyramid becomes larger, larger and takes shape. First we discern a foot on tiptoe, an ankle, a calf, a stretched knee, a taut thigh, a swirling disc of light tulle, a straight slender body, a vertical neck, two arms horizontal like the beam of a balance, and finally a face with a frozen smile and two eyes seeking some point to fix in a fleeting world:

The dancer is born.

She is born out of the whirlwind of music. If the music becomes slower and dies away then the vertical projection that is the dancer will melt away like snow in sunshine. The dust, become dancer, will fall to the ground and shrink back into a little heap of ash.

This is Dance—in its simplicity.

Then our magic box becomes ice-bound again, wrapped in our famous silence.

Soon the silence is gently ruffled, as water is rippled by the passing of an invisible fish.

A Mimer is in the offing.

Now he makes his entry into the room, his chest puffed out before him. His movement rolls the air before him like little boats that lift the water with their prows; from either side two rippling lines form the letter V; he brings a faithful eddy in his wake. He stirs the silence; he creates rhythm, first visual, but then we seem to hear a faint echo of music showing that music has come into being.

This is Mime.

In the art of mime, the first intimation of music is its echo.

If the mimer ceases to operate the music dies, the echo fades away and silence returns. The man is then possessed by the famous ice of our famous silence, like the unhappy Alpine climbers for whom the glacier waits, year after year, to make its own.

Here, in all simplicity, is the difference between mime and dance.

II CONCERNING MIME AND PANTOMIME

The imitation of Nature by gesture is an art as old as Man. The only thing is that books about it do not clutter up our libraries and museums. So it is transmitted with some difficulty. That is its weakness, but also its strength.

Hence we know nothing about the pantomime of the ancients. We know it had bacchic origins, and we think that it was often a burlesque and sometimes obscene.

We don't even know exactly what Deburau's style of panto-mime was like. We can only guess at it across the pantomime we

PLATE VII

ANDRÉ MASSON: Hamlet

PLATE VIII

ETIENNE BERTRAND WEILL: arrangement suggested by *l'Ame et la Danse*
by Paul Valéry

sometimes saw in our childhood thanks to Séverin and, more recently, George Wague.

Apart from these two magnificent examples we have to fall back, as so often happens, on our intellectual intuition.

It is in order to distinguish Séverin's and Wague's art from the more or less artistic results of our own lucubrations that we have called the old type 'Pantomime', and what we have tried to do to-day 'Mime'.

Really pantomime and mime are the same thing—the art of gesture.

But there is an initial difference between the old pantomime (that is to say the pantomime of the second half of the nineteenth century), and contemporary mime.

Pantomime was a *dumb* art; modern mime is a *silent* art.

Ancient pantomime adds to the action proper a gesture language like that of a *dumb man*.

Modern mime, striving after purity, seeks to forswear this dumb language. It aims at being action only, and if it superadds anything it is a sort of lyrical song of gesture; arising from sheer intoxication, the expansion of the soul, what in tragedy is called: the recitative.

What is new in modern mime is its capacity for touching the tragic. It has become a noble art, and that is what entitles it to be compared with Oriental mime. In fact it has nothing of the Oriental. Except that it reaches a level of nobility equivalent to that of Eastern mime.

Therein lies the novelty of Western mime. When our mime 'comes off' it is comparable in beauty to the most beautiful words, to the greatest music, the best painting and the most perfect sculpture.

Until recently pantomime (dumb show) has always been looked on as a popular art, secondary, minor, not a pure art. Modern mime, the *art of silence*, when it succeeds, rises to the level of the fine arts. It is a pure art.

Unfortunately up till now modern mime has seemed to offer only a limited scope. Either it forks off towards the abstract or the

L

abstruse as when explored by someone like Étienne Decroux in his courageous and exemplary labours (Étienne Decroux is the Bernard Palissy of the noblest form of modern mime. Étienne Decroux is the *statuary* of Mime). Or else it harks back to burlesque and links up with ancient pantomime (which is what some mimers younger than us are tending to do with it to-day).

It follows that modern mime has, at least as far as I am concerned, again reached a deadlock. It seems to me in some way to have come to a stop.

Only Charlie Chaplin has reached a pure art based on ancient pantomime. And perhaps the theatre will return to a new form of dumb pantomime drawing from his example. But the fact will still remain that the real problem of modern mime, of pure mime, consists in lifting the art of gesture up to the level of tragedy. As for myself, I hope one day to have the courage to pursue my old dream; I hope to continue my work for the ushering in of *tragic mime*, based on the maxim:

The true and pure expression of this branch of dramatic art is the Art of Gesture.

III   CONCERNING THE ART OF THE WORD

Let us say once more, and then never again!

There are two sorts of word:

The written word,

and the spoken word.

The spoken word is much older than the written word. It is as old as God. It is the 'WORD'. But it does not clutter up our libraries any more than the art of gesture does.

It is the written word that fills our libraries and thus resists the passage of time.

Dramatic art makes essential appeal to the spoken word. That is self-evident. But in order to preserve it throughout the centuries it is put 'into writing'. At the moment when the dramatic poet is inventing, however, there should be no question of writing but only of the *Word*.

Stendhal's 'word' is 'written'. When it is spoken it grates on the tongue. Marivaux's 'word' is 'spoken'; when we speak it the tongue dances. The written French language has a syntax but not a prosody. In the spoken French language the prosody is more important than the syntax.

Moreover it is by the lilt of the phrase, the interplay of the long beat with the short, that the spoken language gets under a man's skin. And it is their breathed quality and plastic density that make consonants and vowels explode in our hearts.

The study of poetry is valuable training for a company.

But it should not be a pretext for showing the actor off; it should be exclusively in the service of the poem. That again is self-evident. The poem should not be acted, and yet it shouldn't be said quite simply, either. What the speaker must do is put himself in the *state* required for saying the poem simply. And this state is achieved by the study of the poet, by love felt for the poet.

It is a sort of state of grace brought about by a concentration of love.

Try to live the poem again, *in the Present,* but without acting it.

Nothing is more difficult. Nothing is more fruitful. Example of a poem characteristic of the interplay of consonants and their plastic precision: Joachim du Bellay's sonnet, *Heureux qui comme Ulysse,* etc.

Example of a poem outstanding for its rhythm, its interplay of long and short beats, the moulding of the syllable and the effect of the sense running over into the next line: *Le Dormeur du Val,* by Rimbaud. . . . Like Ravel.

A company should be able to give recitals of pure poetry. But everything should be known by heart without the help of paper, and the sequence of poems should not be a series of outbursts but a Whole, and this Whole can be of an exceptional poetic power.

There are other exciting ways of studying diction.

You take for instance Debussy's *Pélléas* or one of Glück's operas.

You sing, to a piano accompaniment (it doesn't matter how badly you sing, the important thing is that no one should hear). When you have got hold of the melodic phrasing of the song you try to hang on to that phrasing while leading your voice towards the spoken word.

Finally you are *saying* the words but in accordance with the melodic phrasing of the song.

It is an excellent exercise.

2

The Founding of Our Company

IT was on 1 September, 1946, that the Comédie Française gave
us back our liberty. We were at a serious turning-point in
our lives.

It was now or never to attempt the realisation of our old dream:
to found a company of actors. To own a theatre as one owns a
child.

Or else, as they used to say so rightly in the past: to set up for
oneself. "I set up on my own at such and such an age." "My head
assistant left us this year to set up on his own," etc.

So we decided, Madeleine Renaud and I, to 'set up on our own'.
To found a Theatre. Older friends such as André Brunot, Georges
le Roy, and Catherine Fonteney brought us their support;
younger ones such as Jean Desailly, Jacques Dacqmine, Cattand,
Granval, put their trust in us; friends of our young days such as
M.-H. Dasté, Beauchamp, and Outin joined up with us, followed
to-day by Pierre Brasseur and from time to time by Edwige
Feuillère. Simonne Volterra, the new manager, welcomed us to
the Marigny Theatre.

The 'Compagnie Madeleine Renaud-Jean-Louis Barrault' was
born.

MY 'PARTNER'

If I approached the theatre by tortuous paths, Madeleine
Renaud was thrown into it in the directest possible way. Nothing
was simpler nor more straightforward than her formation.

As a young girl while on holiday at Royan she recited a poem.
De Féraudy was in the room at the time and listened to the
young girl's recitation. When the poem was finished he asked to

see her. He advised the girl's mother to let her daughter study to become an actress.

What was the girl's opinion of it all? She was delighted for she wanted to become 'independent' and earn her living 'by herself'.

So Madeleine asked her mother to let her study for the theatre.

"Very well," said her mother, "but in that case you will go to the Conservatoire and you will enter the Comédie Française; I don't want you to go to the Odéon at any price!"

"Why not the Odéon?"

"Because you would have to cross the Seine and I don't want you to do that."

So Madeleine, the 'ingénue', entered the Conservatoire. She entered with honours and she left with honours. Obedient to her mother she entered the Comédie Française.

And later, when the Odéon was incorporated into the Comédie Française, always obedient to her mother, Madeleine left the Comédie Francaise.

Full stop. That's all.

The rest belongs to Grace. Quality, Art, Soul, Mind; that is not my business.

So Madeleine Renaud received a simple straightforward formation, classical and true.

A formation seemingly opposed, or rather complementary, to the one I had had. The Classical School, the Fauve School. If I seem to be the eternal *Student*, she is the ever-new *Graduate*. The graduate and the student.

Hence we each made our way along opposing paths. So our theatrical association is the encounter of our respective and complementary contributions. Our association is possible because of the similarity of our hearts.

Our hearts resemble each other in this way—both profess a peculiar love for the Human Being. "In the evening of this life we shall be judged on love" (St. John of the Cross). Everything that affects men affects us and puts us into a state of 'sympathy', of communion.

FÉLIX LABISSE: décor for *Occupe-toi Amélie*

163

In this third phase of my life, that is the new thing.

Over and above theories, however passionately interesting, over and above the engrossing problems of technique, we are to-day concerned with the theatre principally as a *human communion.*

It is in this spirit of communion that we have founded the young 'House' that is our Company.

> "On man,
>   By man,
>   For man"

might well be our device. The aim of the theatre, the matter of the theatre, is man, and everything that is or seems to be human in Nature (Animism). The material of the theatre is man; man manufactures theatre (mimicry) and man is the social aim of theatre. So it is for man that we are working.

Hence our association was born under this sign: *the greatest Love of Man.*

CONCERNING THE INFLUENCE OF CERTAIN PEOPLE

To blossom out as men we can either appeal to Grace, or fall back on our instincts, or give ourselves over to passion, or devote ourselves to the glorification of passion while indulging the voluptuous pleasure of analysing it. "The pleasure of glorification is much increased when analysed," said Pascal.

Grace is all very well provided we are of the elect; instinct runs the grave risk of not taking us very far; passion can well be our undoing; and the analysis of passion is a bit arid. Now only man can reconcile these four ways, and that only if he be integrated. He can reconcile Grace and Instinct on the basis of analysed passion. "Lucidity of mind can show you the meaning of your passion", said Pascal, "and that is why a great and lucid mind can love fervently and know distinctly what it is loving." What is excellent is the human realisation of a chamber orchestra, with grace, instinct and passion rising up above a ground base of lucidity, becoming: Music. At the moment when our art is possessed by rhythm, inclined towards music—then it becomes intoxicating.

It is through rhythm and music that we witness the metamorphosis of truth; therein lies style.

Nothing is more intoxicating than to meet in life someone who incarnates our imaginings. Gordon Craig's vague super-marionette, as arid as a robot when perceived only through intellectual speculation, can sometimes be BORN.

There are in fact some people who are, or seem to be, born 'like that'. They are the ELECT. Their art is transposed, with the minimum of loss, into humanity and into truth. They are natural artists; that is to say they can, quite naturally, quit the natural and, like born magicians, bring about the metamorphosis of the true and the human into 'Music'.

This technique alone is to be loved. Our imaginings and love of the theatre can dream no more than that. But whereas some people, barbarian-like, take twisting and brambly paths, the elect have the privilege of the direct way.

The influence they bring is 'Re-birth,' but without renouncing one's aspirations for its sake, nor renouncing belief in one's imaginings, nor betraying what one loves.

Re-birth is what they teach us by their simple and direct example, re-birth towards self-unity, towards the integrating of instinct, passion, analysis, and even Grace.

3

Within the Event

The public thinks that it chooses its
authors; but no. It is the artist who
chooses his public. And one is
always worthy of the other.

ANDRÉ GIDE

A S I draw nearer and nearer to the present time, my reflections, suggested to me by my past most vivid memories,
become rarer and rarer and less and less sure.

We cannot judge of an event while living inside it. A certain
perspective is necessary if we want to see it properly.

For three seasons we have gone on, that's all.

What we must safeguard above all is the Spirit. I can't say that
too often.

It is quite possible that one day in the not too distant future we
shall have to draw in a little for economic reasons. Perhaps we
shall have to give our performances in a workshop or a studio, or
even be a 'number' between two films in a cinema. But if we
have kept our Spirit, our Ideal intact, if we have stayed faithful
to what we love, we shall not have failed.

Perhaps the opposite will happen and one fine day our enterprise will assume vast proportions. On that day more than ever:
watch out for the Spirit!

Yes, either development is possible. I have absolutely no idea
how the Company will evolve. All I know is that it exists, and
that I want to do all I can to ensure it a long life. The external
form doesn't really matter, so long, I repeat, as it remains true
to itself. There again my master, Charles Dullin, sets an example.
Whatever happens to him on the material plane of life, with
regard to his art he preserves a novice's freshness of spirit. 'One

damned thing after another' can befall him, he remains passionately absorbed in an arrangement for a Shakespeare play or a closer interpretation of Molière! What an example of constancy and permanent virginity!

It is possible, like Lugne Poë, to put a play on solely for its literary value and without going to great expense.

It is possible, like Pitoëff, to be sumptuous in poverty and noble within a meagre frame.

It is possible, on the other hand (like Max Reinhart), to preserve simplicity and dignity in the midst of vast productions.

A lot or a little can be thrown into a production. The important thing is to be *honest* and in tune with the *frame* at one's disposal.

It is dishonest to affect poverty when it does not in fact impose itself. Systematic poverty is anyway out of date to-day. Happily! It is unskilful not to conform with the demands of the frame.

It would be dishonest and out of place for us to put *Amphitryon* for example on at the Marigny with impoverished means.

The Marigny is a large frame. It must be filled.

So the choice of lavish or meagre means is not premeditated. It happens automatically:

> according to the play,
> according to the company,
> according to the frame.

There are a hundred ways of mounting a specific play, but only one way given a particular company and a particular frame.

So the problem should be formulated like this: given a particular company and frame, what is the *one proper* way of mounting a specific play?

Le Soulier de Satin, for example, when played within the frame of the Français and with the cast of the Comédie Française, demanded means other than those required, say, in a small theatre and with a company got together for the occasion; and different again from those required in the courtyard of the Sorbonne with the cast of the Théophilien dramatic society.

I am not sure that an author doesn't show different aspects of himself according to the frame and company serving him. The emblem of the theatre is the Kaleidoscope.

The sumptuousness and pomp of Paul Claudel's baroque and supremely Catholic lyricism showed up marvellously in the magnificent frame of the Français. The hard and cruel character of *Le Pain Dur* fitted in perfectly with the Atelier theatre. The verbal starkness of which he is sometimes capable, in *L'Échange*, for example, was well served in the past by the frame of Pitoëff's Mathurins. The poet of love, torn by the problem of the flesh at war with the spirit (as in *Partage de Midi*) suited the Marigny excellently.

Our activity constitutes a sort of five-point star.

> A. Classical authors.
> B. The Art of Gesture.
> C. The Art of Speech.
> · D. Research.
> E. Modern authors.

A. CLASSICAL AUTHORS

The primary function of a classical repertory is to provide *nourishment*.

A good company must be able to interpret the classical theatre.

It is primarily with a view to improving ourselves that we play some of the classics.

The classics provide first and foremost a schooling in style. When we play the classics we have to abandon *naturalism* and yet remain *true* when operating within a particular *tone*. The problem is to find the *tone* and at the same time to remain *true*. The other day I was observing a newspaper-seller. He didn't have to be as it were *present* in his cries because he had found the correct *tone*. If you want to teach someone how to sell papers it is no good telling him to "think carefully about what you're saying". No, he must find the *right tone* and it follows that his cry will produce the *right sound*.

The right tone is the key to style.

There is a Molière tone, a Marivaux tone, a Corneille tone, a Racine tone, a Shakespeare tone, and so on.

And within Molière's plays, for example, there are still further variants of tone. The tone of Amphitryon is musical; the tone of Georges Dandin is realist poetical; the tone of Scapin is almost fishwife, and so on.

The classics, then, improve the style of a company.

A classic is further characterised by its quality of compactness, of *chargedness*. If we divide a picture by an Old Master, say Carpaccio, up into squares and study each square separately we see how loaded the detail is.

In the same way classical dialogue is loaded. Every word is good weight.

The classic demands that we should find the weight of every gesture, every intonation, that we should learn to play *fully*, and capture, in our play, the same sort of chargedness that there is in the text. The interpretation of a part should be divided up into squares, like our picture by Carpaccio, and each section studied for detail; so that the slightest gesture, the most delicate inflection of the voice, may receive its due weight. Its *density*.

If trained like this, a company strikes home and makes a deep impression on the audience.

And side by side with this chargedness, the fountain-head of classical art, the classic teaches *economy*. It makes use of the minimum of means for the maximum yield, and this is because it lives in depth.

Economy is after all less a matter of taste than of concentratedness.

Taste is a tricky and dangerous affair and when discussing economy I prefer to discuss concentratedness rather than good taste.

Before a cat pounces he seems to withdraw into himself; he seems to assemble his resources within himself; dormant. This suggests to me economy in a palpable form.

I remember too the Japanese high-jumpers at the Olympic Games who cleared six and a half feet. Before running almost mechanically towards the bar they too seemed to indulge in a minute's assembling of themselves. They seemed to be lost within themselves. And their leap was all the higher. They skimmed the bar with the maximum of *economy*.

So the classic resists the ravages of Time because of its rightness of tone, its chargedness, its depth and its economy. Because it has gone right to the centre of things, touched the axis. The centre or axis alone is permanent.

The classic starts out from the particular and attains the general.

"Art", says Gide, "lies in painting a particular object with such power that the generality upon which it depends may be grasped."

This is how he makes his own characters. He reveals their general character. He creates the *Function*. The function represents a sort of human type from which depends an infinity of particular people—just as the infinity of points on a circumference depends from one centre.

An actor, by studying the classics, can discover the human type he belongs to, and in that way he can the better serve the characters he is preparing to interpret.

A company versed in the classics is thus easier to cast; and the art of using a company well consists above all in casting it well. If badly cast, a company of good actors can give the appearance of being a bad company. Properly cast, on the other hand, it will give astonishing results. I have known that happen.

Finally, the classical repertory, in its capacity as a crystallised re-creation of mankind, brings us considerable enrichment.

Alas, I am well aware that we do not profit by the experience of others; nevertheless if we knew Shakespeare, Racine and Molière by heart surely we would be the better and the wiser for it.

The poetic perception of Shakespeare, the exacerbated sensibility of Racine, the tragi-comic outlook of Molière—surely these teach us the lesson of things?

PIERRE CABANNE: sketch for *Partage de Midi*

171

That is a summary of the nourishment we can draw from the classics.

Now in what way can a private company serve, in its turn, the classics?

A private company can be useful to the classics because it is a free company. It can look on a classic from an entirely free point of view.

Of course a classic should always be respected. But if it is loved it will automatically be respected. We always respect what we love. And for this very reason it will be respected in the light of love and not in accordance with a list of specifications. A private company can allow itself liberties that a subsidised theatre, custodian of the classical repertory, is denied.

So a private company can shake the classics about a bit at the risk, even, of making mistakes; and yet the shaking brings new life to a classic, spring-cleans it, rejuvenates it.

It also brings *curiosity* to bear on it.

So there can be a mutual exchange of ideas between a private company and a classic, to the benefit of both.

B AND C. THE ART OF GESTURE AND THE ART OF SPEECH

Simultaneously with studying the cream of the Past, the classical repertory, a company should study the art of the Present, and study it to its uttermost limits.

On the extreme left of the art of the theatre stands the art of gesture, or pure mime. On the extreme right stands the art of speech, or pure diction.

We have already given quite enough vent to our preoccupations with these two technical aspects of our art. So we will pass on.

D. RESEARCH

*Treasure-seekers dig much and find
little.*

HERACLITUS

It might well be imagined that by this time every corner of the earth has been explored. No more white blanks on the map of the world.

And yet it appears that there are still some completely unknown regions round about the Orinoco. And that in spite of the march of science and the unconquerable courage and curiosity of some men. So why shouldn't it be the same in the world of the theatre which is after all as old as the earth?

This is the justification for research.

And another thing that justifies it is the fact that the theatre is the art of the Present and that the Present is always *new*.

The study of the classics is a foundation; the study of gesture and diction is a means; the study of the Present, of the ever-new Present, opens up new horizons.

However much a dramatic author may know about man and about the art of using him by voice and gesture, he cannot possibly—because he hasn't the time—drench himself as we do in voice and gesture technique. It follows that he may well overlook some of the resources at his disposal.

And in so far as we can bring light to bear on overlooked resources we can be of service to dramatic authors.

So it is in a '*clinical*' *spirit*, put at the service of modern dramatic authors, that we pursue our researches.

And what enables us to 'work at' dramatic art by crooked paths is the fact that we have, as it were, pure material to work with. It is precisely because the means at our disposal are pure and proper to our art that we can allow our approaches to be *crooked*. This was what we were doing in 1935 when we took *As I Lay Dying* as 'subject-pretext' for showing up the countless resources there are in the bodily expression of a man. And the same in 1937

M

when we tested some of our findings in the service of Cervantes' extraordinary classic, *Numantia*.

The same with Knut Hamsun's *Hunger* in 1939.

And our researches were useful to us in 1943, when we produced Claudel's *Soulier de Satin*. Our researches were valuable to some authors.

Valuable when, with André Gide, we attempted the impossible with Kafka's *Trial*; and more recently still with Camus in *L'État de Siège*.

Perhaps for eight authors out of ten who are uninterested in our findings, there are two who will benefit from them. If so, then our ambition in this field is justified.

But I should confess to a personal joy in these researches, too, over and above the joy of perhaps being of use to living authors.

I must confess that I seized upon the plays mentioned above largely so as to see the kind of performance that I have always wanted to see realised on the stage. There is a certain vision of dramatic art that I would like to see as a spectator. As it is a vision that few authors have, I had to try to tackle the job myself in order to give myself the vision I wanted.

So it is to satisfy the spectator in me that I put on certain 'shows'. And there my ideology could stop.

I am encouraged to press forward along these paths because I was certainly not the only spectator of my kind. (There are many people who have happy memories of *Numantia*, *Hunger* and *The Trial*.)

But first and foremost, by continuing along these lines, there was a good chance of being useful to the living authors I ought to serve and want to serve.

E.   MODERN AUTHORS

Our essential function should be to serve modern authors.

As this section is setting out the very reasons for our existence, it will be brief.

May every author know that we have a place for him. May our state of mind seek to be as broad as possible, as eclectic as possible.

We do not seek to be an author's servant, but his server. Salacrou, Gide, Camus and Claudel have already given us excellent opportunities for serving them. No theatre can exist without the authors who 'feed' it.

It was Dumas, Hugo, C. Delavigne, Balzac who made the Porte Saint-Martin Theatre.

Capus, Labiche, Meilhac and Halévy, R. de Flers made the Variétés.

Coming nearer to our time, Jouvet knows very well what he owes to Giraudoux; Dullin knows what he owes to Jules Romains and Salacrou.

Nearer still, Barsacq knows what he owes to Anouilh.

As for myself I know what I owe to Salacrou and above all to Claudel. And how many others!

Obviously a theatre can bring much to an author; but that is secondary.

The first 'bringing', the one that sets everything going, is the author's.

The author is the CREATOR.

Alongside the authors and the Company, we ourselves dream of forming an intellectual circle round our Company, one that could give us advice if necessary.

Our happiness would be complete if we could bring such a circle into being. A circle, or group, for human communication.

To have ideals in common, to meet together, discuss, sometimes understand each other, give each other the benefit of our knowledge—surely there can be no nobler activity in life.

Christian Bérard, alas, would have been the very spirit of this circle, the symbol of everything I mean by it.

Christian Bérard was stricken and fell in the central alley of the Marigny, falling on his back, his arms outstretched in the shape of a cross, in front of his last décor which he had just finished.

He was carried dying to his home . . . Christian Bérard was the image of a guide, partner and friend.

Bérard died from giving himself. He let himself be drawn in, so gently. He let himself be consumed.

Some days after his funeral one of his faithful friends went to visit his grave and saw that a swarm of bees had settled on the clusters of fading flowers. That is a symbol of Bérard. A whole swarm of bees always settled on Bérard and he let himself be consumed by them. It was thus that he gave his honey to nearly all the *corporations* of Paris.

Whenever Bérard suddenly disappeared, how one sympathised! Having given himself on all sides, he sometimes had to protect himself. But he was always found again and led back by the hand and the demands on him were redoubled.

This was the rule of the serious game he and I played. With Bérard one seemed to go on playing childhood games; that is to say we played with great gravity.

Everyone knows Bérard's work as a décor-maker; everyone knows his contributions to the world of *couture*. Everyone knows the international importance he acquired in those two fields.

His serious painting will become better and better known. But it must never be forgotten that he was provided with antennae of genius. Bérard was the most extraordinary bloodhound I have known. Certainly his judgment showed an excellent intelligence, but there are other models for exceptional intelligence in Paris. Where Bérard was unique was in the way he 'intuited' things. He was (if I may use such a gross comparison) the first Radar made man.

If our work was good, then along came Bérard with Jacinthe, each holding the other on the leash. He had nosed us out. He was on the scent. He was pointing. And we redoubled our efforts.

If there was something wrong with our work . . . Bérard vanished. No one knew where he was. Bérard was absent. It was a bad sign. And he didn't do it deliberately. On the contrary. No, Bérard was quite simply the barometer of quality.

He never made a mistake.

This gift filled me with admiration. It passes understanding. It is instinct at the service of the intelligence.

Bérard brought us a great deal. *Amphitryon, Scapin.* Ysé's dresses in *Partage de Midi*. It is above all the counsellor that we will perhaps never find again.

May his memory be the emblem of the Group we hope to form round our Company.

To sum up: from the classics we seek nourishment.

Through the study of gesture and speech we hope to perfect our technique.

By periodic excursions into the unknown we hope to enrich ourselves.

And all *in the service of modern authors.*

That is, it seems to us, our function.

So that is our activity.

AS I LAY DYING TO PARTAGE DE MIDI

When I have no more strength left
I shall stop.

ANTIGONE

It happened that when in 1935 we presented a dramatic action drawn from *As I Lay Dying,* it served as a manifesto for the rehabilitation of the art of gesture.

But my first production might equally well have been a manifesto for a particular form of the spoken word. And in that case I would have chosen Claudel's *Partage de Midi*.

But actually *Partage de Midi* is our most recent production.

There is a vast and profound study to be written on Paul Claudel as a playwright.

When we put on Claudel's *Partage de Midi* I had for the second time in my life the strange and sublime feeling that I was putting on a future classic.

While we were working on *Partage de Midi*—Edwige Feuillère, P. Brasseur, J. Dacqmine and myself—we couldn't help imagining the deep but agonising joy the seventeenth-century actors must have had when working on *Bajazet* or *Britannicus* for the first time under Racine's supervision.

I had felt this joy once before when producing *Le Soulier de Satin*, but with *Partage de Midi* we were working at the very core of Claudel's *théâtre*. The crucible where the poet, himself in the noonday of his life, had undergone the ordeal by Fire. The crucible from which he was afterwards to rise up, metamorphosed.

Partage is the inner ring towards which the 'early-manner' works converge (those published by the *Mercure de France* under the general title "L'Arbre"), and from which there springs a strong shoot pointing upwards toward his personal victory, of which the synthesis, twenty-five years later, was to be precisely *Le Soulier de Satin*.

The real and the unreal,

The visible and the invisible,

The world that you can read 'like a book', and the reverse side of the book—all these live mysteriously side by side in *Partage*, and just when the poet and his characters are going to pass from the one to the other, we find: "*Ame outrée sortie de son corps, comme une épée à demi dégainée!*"

In *Partage de Midi* the Claudel of *Tête d'Or* remains with his human physical power intact, and yet the power is withdrawing a little towards the sublimation that will lift Claudel's Catholic genius up towards the perfect fulfilment of *Le Soulier de Satin*.

What deep happiness for me to have been able to enter into the *real* drama of Paul Claudel's life, to have heard his most human cries, by means of this grinding, sorrowful key—*Partage de Midi*.

★

If it were possible for us to polarise dramatic art as we polarise light, *As I Lay Dying* would be at the extreme left of the dramatic spectrum, and *Partage de Midi* would be at the extreme right.

Dramatic art extends between these two extremes: pure gesture, pure speech.

And beside Claudel, *Phèdre*,
And beside Faulkner, *Hunger*,
With Shakespeare and Molière in the middle.

So dramatic art becomes a rainbow, "a rainbow woven with a hundred silks", as La Fontaine said.

As I Lay Dying
   Hunger
      The Trial
         L'État de Siège
            Nuits de la Colère
             Numantia
               Antony and Cleopatra
               Hamlet
                Les Fourberies de Scapin
              Les Fausses Confidences
           La Seconde Surprise de l'Amour
      Amphitryon
    Phèdre
Partage de Midi

In fourteen years fourteen plays by means of which we have travelled—for a first time—over the cycle of dramatic art.

All that remains is for us to go on.

The Theatre is first and foremost an art in motion. Everything must always be wiped out, forgotten, so that we can start again.

It is a permanent revolution. There lies its passionately interesting side. Every day we have to be born again. There's the rub.

There is no point in going on explaining.

My confidences have come to an end, and the various reflections suggested by my memories.

Now I am going to return to action, the sole purpose of my life.

I have finished, then.

And now I shall try to forget what I have written. "Forgive the author's mistakes", as they say on the Spanish stage.

I shall appeal to Robert Desnos for the summing up of my present state of mind. It was one of the last sentences he wrote:

AND NOW
TELL ME ABOUT THE
ADVENTURES OF MEN

Cap Camarat, June, 1949.

Index

CONTRACT LAW IN AN E-COMMERCE AGE

UNITED KINGDOM
Sweet & Maxwell Ltd
London

AUSTRALIA
LBC Information Services Ltd
Sydney

CANADA and USA
Carswell
Toronto

NEW ZEALAND
Brooker's
Wellington

SINGAPORE and MALAYSIA
Sweet & Maxwell
Singapore and Kuala Lumpur